A Family Casebook: Problem-Based Learning and Mindful Self-Reflection

Maria Napoli
Arizona State University

Boston   New York   San Francisco

Mexico City   Montreal   Toronto   London   Madrid   Munich   Paris

Hong Kong   Singapore   Tokyo   Cape Town   Sydney

Editor-in-Chief, Social Sciences: Karen Hanson
Senior Series Editor: Patricia Quinlin
Series Editorial Assistant: Nakeesha Warner
Marketing Manager: Laura Lee Manley
Production Supervisor: Liz Napolitano
Editorial Production Service: Pine Tree Composition, Inc
Composition Buyer: Linda Cox
Manufacturing Buyer: Joanne Sweeney
Electronic Composition: Pine Tree Composition, Inc
Cover Administrator: Elena Sidorova

For related titles and support materials, visit our online catalog at www.ablongman.com.

Between the time website information is gathered and then published, it is not unusual for some sites to have closed. Also, the transcription of URLs can result in typographical errors. The publisher would appreciate notification where these errors occur so that they may be corrected in subsequent editions.

Library of Congress Cataloging-in-Publication Data

Napoli, Maria.
    A family casebook : problem-based learning and mindful self-reflection / Maria Napoli.
        p. cm.
    Includes bibliographical references and index.
    ISBN 0-205-37943-5
    1. Family psychotherapy—Case studies. I. Title.
    [DNLM: 1. Family Therapy—Case Reports. 2. Family Therapy—Problems and Exercises. WM 18.2 N216f 2007]
    RC488.5.N365 2007
    616.89'156—dc22

                                                      2006024129

Printed in the United States of America

10   9   8   7   6   5   4   3   2   1   10   09   08   07   06

For my mother Mary who taught me that the foundation of unconditional family love is the glue that binds the heart. For my father Al, siblings Bobby, Lisa, and Pamela and sons, Eric and David who have shared my life challenges and joys throughout our journey of life.

CONTENTS

iv

ACKNOWLEDGMENTS

The writing of this family casebook has been like weaving the threads of art, heart, and knowledge into a unified whole. I thank all of the families who have shared their stories and have offered an invaluable learning opportunity for students. I thank my formal and informal mentors and reviewers, Hank Radda, William Mermis, Tamara Rounds, Elizabeth Segal, and Rena Gordon. They have provided inspiration and suggestions and have guided my creative vision. A special thanks to the talented therapists who contributed engaging and interesting family cases: Paul Rock Krech, Tamara Rounds, Renay Segal, and Bart Miles. A large round of applause and gratitude to Valarie Piaciatelli, a gifted artist and therapist who contributed all of the artwork for the family cases. Each piece of art depicts her careful and keen insight into the family stories.

A very special thanks to Sarah Trachtenberg, who spent her summer working with me, transferring my notes and handwritten manuscript to the computer. Thanks to Mary Lutes, who unfailingly helped put the manuscript together, making copies, organizing artwork, and attending to the final details before the manuscript was shipped to the editor. Thanks to Pat Quinlin, my editor, who was supportive and answered many questions however redundant and simplistic and kept me on track throughout the writing of this book. Last but not least, a warm thank you to my sons, Eric and David, who were patient and understanding while I spent days in my office writing this book and who helped in the final stages of organization before the manuscript was sent to the editor.

Introduction

A Note to Students

The field of family therapy has changed over the last few decades for both therapist and client. The early family theorists, Ackerman, Bowen, Minuchin, Haley, and Satir, are a few pioneers who have given us a framework for family therapy. Many early theorists were trained in psychoanalysis, which was the foundation of the early family therapy models. Today, many family therapists use a blend of family therapy theories, incorporate personal style in therapy, and view the family in an integrated model that considers the impacts of culture, gender, environment, spiritual practices, health, nutrition, and lifestyle on the family.

Understanding the relationship among thoughts, feelings, and the physical body and learning how to be present through mindfulness have offered therapists more opportunities to support families and create change in families' lives. During the first several decades of family therapy, therapists spent many hours in training, during which they were evaluated and supervised. Unfortunately, today there is often limited time available to train therapists and decreased time for individual supervision. Managed care and the increase in therapists' caseloads have impacted the quality of care families receive.

This family casebook is written to help you understand the family therapy process in a lifelike setting. It walks you through each case from intake to termination and offers you the opportunity to explore various theoretical models while evaluating and developing your clinical skills. Creating a space for self-reflection while working in small groups sets the stage for you to receive peer supervision and understand how you will function in the family treatment session. The adventure you are about to embark upon in reading this casebook will offer you the opportunity to explore and process family stories and your personal transformation through a problem-based learning approach and mindful self-reflection. This family casebook is written to give you a fundamental toolbox for family therapy while creating opportunities for exploration of theory, culture, and self.

Problem-Based Learning

A problem-based learning (PBL) approach uses real problems to engage you in the subject (for our purpose, family cases), which facilitates the development of effective critical thinking and communication skills. The real-life cases are interesting problems that stimulate curiosity and challenge you to rethink assumptions while remaining present with the family. Literature notes that relative to a conventional lecture-based curriculum, "PBL curricula improves student problem solving skills, enhances understanding and retention of basic science concepts and improves performance in clinical clerkships." (Anderson & Glew, p. 2) In a problem-based learning classroom, you are better able to transfer knowledge gained because you are the master of your experience through exploration and research. "One of the arguments used to support the superiority of PBL is the concept of contextual learning. The basic premise is that when we learn material in the context of how it will be used, it promotes learning and the ability to use the information" (Albanese, 2000, p. 733).

There are three essential elements in the PBL approach:

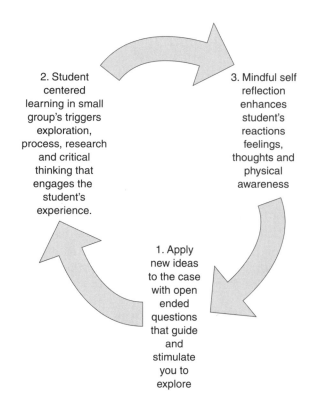

2. Student centered learning in small group's triggers exploration, process, research and critical thinking that engages the student's experience.

3. Mindful self reflection enhances student's reactions feelings, thoughts and physical awareness

1. Apply new ideas to the case with open ended questions that guide and stimulate you to explore

In PBL environments, you act as a professional and confront problems as they occur, with fuzzy edges and insufficient information, and you explore various solutions to the family's challenges. It is in the process of struggling with the family's actual problems that you learn both content and critical thinking skills. An important benefit of PBL is that you engage fully in the process and thus gain experience during your early training to take responsibility for your learning. Professionals are often left to self-discipline and independent learning; therefore, experience in a PBL classroom will prepare you to become an effective family therapist.

Mindful Self-Reflection

*Less and less do I give energy to the doing of counseling. Now
I seek stillness, to pay attention, be there—the almost impossible
which, when it occurs, produces a miracle, and a celebration.*
Sweet, 1989, p. 6

Family therapists are at high risk for becoming enmeshed, overidentified with, and caught up in family interactions during the clinical session. Whether you are a recent or seasoned family therapist, your feelings. opinions, biases, and personal history continually play a role in the therapeutic relationship. To assist you in maintaining clear boundaries and objectivity as well as remaining present for the family, you will take time throughout the family story for mindful self-reflection.

What is mindfulness? Mindfulness is bringing attention to your present experience without judgment on purpose. It is a state in which you not only have experiences but you are also able to observe the ongoing contents of your experiences without interference. Mindfulness fosters open communication between the unconscious and the conscious. For example, you meet an old friend in a coffee shop, a strange feeling emerges in your stomach, and you ignore the physical sensation. When you leave the coffee shop you find that you are irritated yet you are not aware of the reason. Let's try that scenario again. You meet your friend in the coffee shop and pay attention to sensations in your stomach and suddenly are aware of some uncomfortable feelings you have toward the friend; you acknowledge them to yourself and understand more fully what is going on at the moment. Simply noticing is the goal.

Mindfulness is nonjudgmental, self-reflective consciousness in action. The therapist's mindful self-reflection throughout each case facilitates keen awareness of the therapy process. To participate effectively in a relationship with clients, you need to understand how you contribute to the interactions. Therapists who are able to focus on being in the moment and maintaining a loving presence increase the opportunity for awareness of what is occurring and hence increase their capacity for empathy.

In therapy, strong emotions are sometimes felt and early memories come back with intensity and clarity. When we are mindful, these experiences can be examined and used to free us from the painful unconscious compulsion to repeat these feelings and memories again and again. When we examine sensations in our bodies and thoughts in the midst of the session, we can discover in them the roots of who we are and how we got that way. When clients are mindful, they can turn attention inward, quiet the mind, and notice the emergence of feelings, thoughts, body sensation, and images. By paying attention to their experience in the present, clients can view old feelings and thoughts in a new and novel way.

A significant difference between working with families and individuals is that as therapists we must connect with the process of not only one person but of each individual family member, and be able to connect the process of those individuals with each other. Thoughts and reactions become intensified when as therapists we become bombarded with feelings toward multiple family members during the session. When therapists are mindful, they increase objectivity and are better able to deal with their counter-transference, personal feelings and thoughts that emerge, by responding to them without judgment. Finally, it is important for us when working with families to listen to the storytellers and not the story. Instead of trying to "fix" the problem, you are encouraged to explore and learn the art of spontaneity, of being present to the client's experience.

Format of Family Cases: Twelve Core Ingredients in the Family Story

The following list illustrates how each family case is developed in this book. Each section gives you ample opportunity to process and explore how you will approach treatment by evaluating the family dynamics and the family story as well as your personal process of understanding what is happening to you during treatment. In addition, there are guides that offer information regarding the issues presented in each case as well as simple activities to help rejuvenate, relax, and stimulate your body and senses, which prevents burnout and increases awareness and objectivity. Each section takes you through the case, step by step, which makes the treatment experience more lifelike. There is no specific diagnosis or theoretical model suggested. Each student will make his or her own assessment regarding treatment, and each student will provide input based on his or her clinical style, personality, and technique in regard to theoretical frameworks and practice tools. You will have ample opportunity to make observations in each phase of treatment, which will lead to more questions and stimulate your curiosity, engagement, creativity, and cultural awareness. Let's explore the ingredients of our problem-based learning format and how we will be using this approach in our book.

About the Family Case

1. *Getting Started*—Each case begins with pertinent information regarding the presenting problem. Students will assess what might be going on with the family by exploring their ideas and answering open-ended questions that lead to an initial assessment.

2. *A Window into the Past*—This section offers the student a historical perspective of each family member. Students will have the opportunity to explore family patterns and causes for issues presented and gain a broader picture of each family member. Students will answer questions regarding the history presented, which will offer an opportunity to generate more questions and reflect upon reactions, feelings, and opinions about the family.

3. *Embracing the Essence*—The key issues regarding the case are explored. Students make an assessment of what is going on and how they might deal with the family. Students answer questions that will assist them in making a comprehensive assessment while generating more questions to follow their perceptions.

4. *Celebrating Family Culture*—Students discuss how culture shapes the family story. This section will open up dialogue in two areas, the traditional norms of that culture and how the family integrates the culture with their personal lifestyle, issues confronting them, values, and beliefs. Students have the opportunity to process thoughts and generate questions about the family's culture.

5. *Riding the Wave*—Students explore various interventions and treatment plans based on the case thus far. Excerpts from sessions and group exploration all contribute to developing ideas for intervention and treatment techniques that can assist in creating change in the family.

6. *Beyond Treatment*—The goal of termination in treatment is to empower families to use the tools learned in therapy. develop their own tools, and process the next step for them after they leave treatment. Students explore issues that will continue to facilitate the family's growth and transformation and will offer tools and suggestions for the family's well-being after treatment.

About the Therapist

7. *Mindful Self-Reflection Moment*—Through the therapist's mindful self-reflection, keen awareness of what is occurring in the therapist's process unfolds. Students take a reflective moment to explore their personal feelings, opinions, and reactions. To establish the cooperation of the unconscious, the therapist must be able to let go of any need to be doing only what he or she wants to do. That's not as easy as it may sound. Our thoughts and behavior are not always conscious or controllable. The therapist's ability to become aware of and accept thoughts and behaviors

without judgment is an indication of great maturity. The key to practicing mindfulness is the ability to listen to your intuition, your sense of knowing through your thoughts, body, and senses.

8. *Take a One-Minute Vacation*—Therapists often do not take a break between sessions or during the day to nurture themselves, clear out thoughts, stretch the body, replenish energy, and simply breathe. Taking a one-minute vacation offers simple tools to step back and take a break to increase sensory awareness, relaxation, and energy. (All of the suggested one-minute vacation activities were taken from *Tools for Balanced Living: A Mindfulness Practice Workbook,* by Maria Napoli, vision@visiongraphics.com.)

About the Therapist's Clinical and Research Guides

9. *Exploratory Research and Resource Corner*—Student groups discuss and assign tasks to each other for additional resources, family homework, and readings needed to proceed with family treatment. For example, the group may decide to develop a genogram and have each member of the family write a biography of other family members. This assignment offers each family member an opportunity to "dance in the shoes" of each other. Another tool for empowering the family are "recognition days": a homework assignment in which the family members tell each other every day one or more positive feelings they may have toward each other (e.g., saying thank you or acknowledging good behavior). It helps to have family members reflect what feels good and supports them. Exchanging positive feelings and actions increases family awareness and empathy.

   These homework assignments facilitate the family members' engagement and participation in their treatment. They also offer families the opportunity to try out new behaviors, experience small changes, and describe feelings and thoughts when they are in session together. This section gives students an opportunity to be creative in developing homework assignments, consult resources that offer knowledge about the family, and use critical thinking skills through research.

10. *Therapist's Tools*—Ideas and suggestions regarding clinical issues and treatment techniques are discussed, offering students the opportunity to "try on" different practice skills and reflect upon pertinent clinical and personal themes that emerge in treatment.

11. *Thoughts to Ponder*—Information regarding pertinent themes in the family case is offered to give students additional opportunities to make assessments, interventions, plan treatment, and stimulate critical thinking.

12. *Expanding your Knowledge*—This section enables students to increase their knowledge about issues confronting the family. Students can research articles and books for their student group and exploratory and research corners as well as gain knowledge for future use.

Let's now review three core ingredients necessary in treating families and how you can integrate these in working with the families in your family casebook.

Integrative Family Therapy

Insanity is doing the same thing over
and over and expecting different results.
Albert Einstein

Let's take a closer look at how problem-based learning and mindfulness impact the family therapy process. The problem-based learning approach presented in this book will take you out of a cookie-cutter model. It offers opportunities to explore how you will function for each family and family member while mindfully paying attention to the present. Instead of reading the family story in its entirety and then answering questions, you will be fully engaged in each aspect of the treatment, which mirrors family therapy in real life. Four key ingredients to take into consideration in working with families are safety, discovery, working in the moment, and treating the client holistically.

Every session, indeed every relationship, is a dance between the therapist and client. We are often unaware of our part in the dance, such as when personal thoughts and feelings interfere with the present experience, what's happening now. The core of healing takes place not only in the family's discovery but in the family–therapist relationship/dance. To create change in the family, you need to create a safe environment, be available to discover with the family, maintain a loving presence, let go of rigid thinking, see the family as a holistic entity, and engage the body, senses, spiritual, emotional, and psychological aspects of yourself and the family.

Safety

The key to developing a successful relationship with clients who seek treatment is safety. When a client is not feeling safe, defenses peak, which blocks the ability for clients to go inside and learn about those parts of themselves that need protection. Ultimately, the goal of treatment is discovering possibilities, reframing limiting beliefs, and exploring new options. Therapists can create the environment for clients toward this transformation through mindfulness by paying close attention to and acknowledging the moment-to-moment internal experience of the family by listening to behavior, postures, gestures, and tensions among family members. Mindfulness allows experiences to be noticed because the therapist is willing to look at clients and see whatever is there, whether it be pain, joy, or fear.

Discovery

Clients need to be assisted in discovering that guidance and understanding are inside themselves. Faith in each person's ability to find the necessary answers and tools within is extremely empowering. It is the job of the family therapist to connect with the unconscious and create a setting in which these emotions can emerge in the conscious state of mindfulness.

Working in the Moment

Family therapy comes to life when working with the present experiences of family members. When everyone—therapist and clients—is present, there is no longer a need to guess about motivations or possible interpretations for behavior. Instead, there is engagement in developing each family member's ability to be connected with self and with each other. Instead of discussing change, family members can take actual risks by trying out new behaviors and beliefs in the session.

People want to change desperately, yet at the same time they resist change. We long for freedom from our limitations yet are afraid to let go of old behaviors and thoughts that no longer serve us. Fear of the unknown is often more powerful than the possibility of change. When the therapist blocks his or her own feelings, the therapist consciously or unconsciously supports an avoidance strategy in the client, and this prevents change.

When therapists are mindful, they become available for empathic mirroring, an essential therapeutic technique. Reflecting back a family member's immediate internal experience is very intimate and lets the family know that the therapist is present with the family in a deep way. Working with immediate experience provides both the therapist and family with the opportunity to access feelings more readily. In short, experience, wisdom, humanness, and personal development are vital if healing is to occur.

Holistic Perspective

When we pay attention to the whole person, it is possible to see who we are "dancing with." Family members' personalities are expressed in their tone of voice, gestures, posture, and idiosyncratic behaviors that mark them as unique. When the therapist evokes experiences that lead to the core issues and then helps the client process the experience in the session, transformation takes place. Teaching clients energizing and relaxing breathing exercises and facilitating body awareness by progressive relaxation and stretching can help clients listen to their physical cues and lead them to more information about how they experience certain situations. Creating exercises that stimulate the senses and listening without judgment to clients' intuition enhance the integration of the whole person and offer a rich, comprehensive, and powerful experience that facilitates awareness and transformation.

Goals of Therapy

1. Assist families to mindfully observe their own experiences and stories by creating a safe and trusting atmosphere.
2. Empower families to explore challenges and develop alternatives to behaviors and beliefs that keep them stuck and consequently block transformation.
3. Reinforce therapist and family awareness through mindful self-reflection by listening deeply to instincts, body, and feelings.

Example of an excerpt of a family session (Mom; Dad; Mary, fifteen years old; and Tommy, eleven years old. Seating arrangement: Dad, Mom, Mary, Tommy, and therapist).

MARY: (Speaking to therapist.) My father never talks to me. He complains to mom about me and then yells at me for stupid things.

DAD: (Looks at mom.) This is ridiculous; I'm always trying to talk to her and she's usually locked in her room.

THERAPIST: I'm hearing that you have attempted to communicate with Mary. Would it be OK if we create an opportunity for communication right now? Dad, can you go over and sit next to Mary?

DAD: (Nervously moves over to sit next to Mary, arms folded across his chest.)

THERAPIST: (Turns to dad.) Before you say anything, can you take a moment to listen to how your body feels right now and anything else you are aware of? Take your time, turn your attention inward, and notice any thoughts, feelings, sensations, changes in your breathing, tension or relaxation, memories, or images that arise. (Therapist slows voice down and closes eyes in order to model turning attention inward.)

(Everyone waits for a very long minute or two.)

THERAPIST: Dad, can you tell us what's happening?

DAD: (Facial expression softens.) I don't know what just happened. My stomach feels knotted and I feel a little afraid.

THERAPIST: Can you tell us more about being afraid?

DAD: It's weird, I thought of my father yelling at me and how scared I was. Mary reminds me of him.

MARY: (Reaches out and touches Dad's hand.)

DAD: (Responds and holds hand.)

Notice here that the job of the therapist is to help the client's inner wisdom unveil itself rather than to provide advice or answers. In this way, clients learn not to depend on an external authority for answers but to tap their own resources and capacity for healing. Our job of therapist becomes much simpler because we don't need to have all the answers, yet more challenging because guiding clients inward to their own healing potential requires awareness.

There's a difference between discussing chocolate candy and eating it, between walking on the beach and thinking about it. By working with live experience, one performs psychotherapy in vivo as opposed to in vitro. People develop psychological difficulties not just as the result of discussion, but because of the impact of real experiences; therefore, it is very important to create real experiences in psychotherapy as opposed to simply talking about them. We give clients ample tools toward congruity when feelings, thoughts, senses, and movement match their experience. Here are some tools to guide family members toward awareness of their present experience.

Inner body sensations: Breath, heart rate
Senses: Smells, taste, sight, touch, hearing, body temperature, and intuition
Movement: Posture, facial expressions, trembling, gestures
Affect: Emotions, fear, joy, anger, or sadness
Cognition: Thoughts, beliefs

Enjoy your professional and personal journey!

A Note for Teachers

This family case study book uses a problem-based learning (PBL) format and mindful self-reflection. The combination of these tools will facilitate critical thinking, creativity, group cohesiveness, clinical skill development, and self-awareness. The intention of problem-based learning is that the students start from a place of not knowing. The first step is for them to be able to identify what they don't know. Students are presented with segments of a family case scenario that is somewhat ill structured and not too specific, to get them to start thinking, develop some ideas, and consider what more they need to know to work effectively with the family. This learning approach was first introduced in medical school education. Blake, Hosokawa and Riley (2000) examined students' performances on step 1 and step 2 of the United States Medical Licensing Examination following the implementation of a problem-based learning curriculum and found that the mean scores were higher on the USMLE step 1 for classes in the problem-based learning curriculum than classes in the traditional curriculum. The mean scores for step 2 were above the national mean for classes in the revised curriculum and below the national mean for classes in the traditional curriculum. (2000, p. 66) Students could memorize extensively yet had difficulty transferring the information to diagnose diseases. The "feeding tube" style of teaching did not offer students the opportunity to process information learned, which is a key ingredient in transferring knowledge from one situation to another, the classroom to the treatment room. Kwan notes that "the true spirit of PBL is for teachers to become effective facilitators (as tutors) and teachers (as resource persons), by providing feedback and guidance to their performance in facilitating learning and handling group dynamics, and by giving them attractive incentives and rewards." (Kwan, 2000, p. 2)

The family cases in this book give students a lifelike clinical experience of treating a family from the intake interview through termination. While participating in the PBL approach, students can process family treatment issues in each phase of the case while working in groups discussing treatment issues in the following sections: Getting Started—the initial interview; Embracing the Essence—assessment; Riding the Wave—intervention and treatment; and Beyond Treatment—termination and prevention.

Family therapists have always realized the significance of family history and how it relates to present behavior. The section A Window into the Past offers students a peek at where the family has been historically. Family therapists realize the need to be more informed not only about a family's behavioral history but about the significant role culture plays in shaping a family's life. The section Celebrating Family Culture offers students an opportunity not only to explore cultural history and norms but to examine how acculturation, oppression, disability, and gender have impacted a family's life.

There are three sections that offer students information to better understand the issues confronting the family. Exploratory Research and Resource guides students to explore the literature, to consult with outside professionals, and to develop homework assignments that will empower families and assist them in creating change. Thoughts to Ponder are snapshots of information that shed light on the issues the family is confronting. Therapist's Tools is designed to offer students practice tips in working with the family. Therapist's Mindful Self-Reflection moment offers students a time to check in with themselves and how they are functioning with the family. Practicing mindfulness, being aware of the present experience without judgment, enables students to become more aware of how they affect the therapy process. This mindful self-awareness enables students to "get out of their own way." They are then able to increase objectivity, listen without judgment, and facilitate transformation for themselves and the family.

Ideally, PBL students work in small groups of five to seven. Students will initially get very little information. In the family case story the initial information provided is the presenting problem and the client's situation. The scenario will evolve in response to the various input of members of the group. Whatever is done will be based on reality, and it is authentic in that it reflects what students will be exposed to when they experience professional practice.

There are a number of reasons to use PBL. Some students feel that they need to solve a problem and want someone to give them a prescription for how to solve this problem instead of processing the issues themselves. Working in a group, formulating and exchanging ideas, and asking questions while reading the family story help students to develop skills for real practice. PBL students are becoming recognized as skilful communicators because they must communicate what they learn to their teammates on a continuing basis. They are also becoming recognized as more active learners as a result of each group member being accountable for opinions and skill during the students' group discussion; in addition, peer pressure from teammates provides extra incentives for PBL students.

Characteristics of a PBL Student

- Commitment to self/student-directed learning.

- Active participation in discussion and critical thinking while contributing to a friendly, nonjudgmental environment.

- Willingness to make a constructive evaluation of self and group members.

- Teamwork and effective communication skills are valued.

Problem-based Learning and Family Cases

One important characteristic of a good learning case is that the family case be engaging. When students work through a family learning case, they will be eager to find out any related information to help them understand the case; the case should capture their interest. Family learning cases do not always have a solution; thus solving the problem is not the ultimate goal of problem-based learning. Instead, the family case serves as a learning vehicle. Cases need to have specific learning outcomes embedded in them. In small groups a family case is read, group members identify the "facts" they know—information inherent in the family case. Students express their "ideas"—hypotheses or thoughts—about why they think these facts in the family case are important. Next, students identify their "learning needs"—what they need to learn to find out whether their ideas are valid. Students then go to a variety of learning resources, agencies, hospitals, clinics, the Web sites, libraries, and experts to acquire the information needed.

Characteristics of Problem-Based Family Cases

- Students come in "cold" to the case.

- The case is engaging and holds the students' attention and stimulates the students to explore avenues of assessment and treatment.

- Students will initially receive some information about the case in the section Getting Started.

- The case follows with progressive disclosure, whereby the case unfolds step by step.

- Cases present open-ended questions without simplistic cookie-cutter answers.

- This unfolding initiates active discussion and leads to the next step in the case.

- Questions are posed to students during each phase of the case, which leads students to read and do research to obtain information that will lead to the next phase.

- Students determine the learning issues and follow up within their group.

- There are enough issues to stimulate in-depth discussions and study.

Benefits of Problem-Based Learning for Family Cases

- Students face challenging problems, yet in a safe environment in which they can solve those problems together, generate questions, and receive feedback.

- Students learn to analyze complex problems and how to perform critical thinking and research to confront the problems or test their treatment approaches and ideas.

- Students are faced with certain aspects of the family case, and in solving them they acquire theoretical and practical skills.

- Students learn group skills, improve their negotiation abilities, and learn to listen, develop communication skills, and assess their role in the group.

- PBL stimulates creative thinking, enhances flexibility, and allows students to be in the moment as they tap into their own resources to find solutions.

- Students depend upon each other for guidance to come up with the best possible solution for the family.

As the teacher, your role is to facilitate discussion. You are a guide, helping students to draw upon their own perceptions, experiences, and knowledge through discussion, research, and dialogue with peers and the teacher. For example, when learning needs are identified in a family case, each member will take a small portion of the learning tasks and become "master" of those tasks. Students then come back to help their teammates understand where, what, and how they learned the information obtained.

Characteristics of a Good PBL Facilitator

There are no special skills for learning to use the problem-based learning approach other than being available to partner with students in the learning process. "Teachers serving as tutors are not knowledge providers as in the case of spoon-feeding; they serve to facilitate the learning process. Instructions are carried out via discussions among students in small group tutorial format." (Kwan, 2000, p. 2) The problem-based learning approach takes the pressure off of you to be "on" at all times, which often occurs with lecturing. Problem-based learning creates an atmosphere for you to interact and exchange ideas and knowledge with students, hence increasing classroom participation, interest, and motivation to learn. In addition, you have less concern about students who are shy and withdrawn and those who monopolize and control since students are in small groups that are set up for mutual participation. This offers all students the opportunity to increase their ability to integrate knowledge, test clinical skills, and learn from peers without judgment. Problem-based learning makes teaching a fun experience! It involves the following:

- Commitment to student-directed learning

- Acceptance of the role of developing good questioning skills

- Ability to provide a safe learning environment while facilitating discussion and critical thinking

- Willingness to make a constructive evaluation of students and group processes

- Ability to stimulate, guide, and question, when necessary, to make sure learning issues are identified, researched, and discussed

Facilitating a Family Story

The following ten points offer you a template for organizing the problem-based learning classroom using the family stories in this book. Based on class size and time available for each class, you will plan according to your schedule. Each case can be discussed anywhere from one to six hours depending upon the depth of discussing clinical interventions, skills, and issues that arise and discussing family theory and other clinical diagnoses, cultural implications, and research discovered. Note that students can read the cases at home and answer all of the questions and process their responses in the small groups. This can save time for shorter class schedules, yet still offer the benefits of using the PBL approach. A unique aspect of this book is that undergraduate, graduate, doctoral-level students, and seasoned therapists can work with the family stories at different levels of practice skill. Here are some tips.

1. Students form small groups.
2. Have each group respond to the initial statement made by the family member in the Getting Started section. (Note that a student's first reaction to the client offers an opportunity to process how those reactions might impact treatment)
3. Discuss students' reactions/responses with the class.
4. Students return to their groups to answer questions and give feedback in the Getting Started section regarding the family and student's mindful self-reflection
5. Bring the student groups together to share responses and give your feedback. Engage in class discussion.
6. Students return to their group and move to the next phase of the family story, Window into the Past.
7. Student groups continue to process each section of the case.
8. Students bring results of their process for discussion with teacher and rest of students.
9. When the class ends for the day, students assign tasks to each group member for the next class
10. Students and teacher give a synthesis of what has occurred in class, offers suggestions, and give feedback.

In summary, your teaching journey of using a problem-based learning approach and mindful self-reflection will offer you a quality teaching experience in which both you and your students exchange ideas and participate in the process of riding the wave of family treatment together. Teaching should be fun for teachers as well as students. Embrace the transformation together!

Future Directions of the Family

Over time, the family has functioned as a holistic unit. Everything that occurred was centered around contributing to the health and sustainment of the family. Women gathered in groups of extended family to garden, cook, sew, and care for children; men gathered to farm, hunt, and build. Meals were eaten together in large family groups. Mentors for children came in all sizes with wisdom offered in a multitude of areas. We did not hear much about depression, isolation, attention deficit hyperactivity disorder (ADHD), burnout, or addiction. Each person in the family often had many eyes on him or her, and this functioned as a built-in prevention system.

Today, families have become smaller, and as a result of technology and travel, many live miles away from extended family, and children are more isolated, have fewer mentors and models, and often are not physically in contact with loving human beings, a key ingredient for the survival of the human spirit. The high incidence of disease and focus on symptom reduction rather than cure and the devastating increase in family violence have brought us full circle to try and recapture and remember the days of yesterday, when there was plenty of love to go around. Modern families are increasingly searching for a connection through community group support, group activities for children, and visiting with family and friends more often. We are trying to nurture the health and our bodies through exercise, organic foods, clean water, and a movement toward relaxation and recreation.

There is hope for our modern-day family as we feel the pains of individual and family challenges that impact our lives.

As family therapists, we, too, have and must become models of health for those we treat. Taking time out for lunch, peer supervision, mindful self-reflection, relaxation practices, and play is essential for nurturing our humanness. These gifts we offer to ourselves are gifts shared with the families we work with; in this way, we all benefit through movement toward a better quality of life, a life filled with love and acceptance.

REFERENCES

Albanese, A. (2000). Problem-based learning: why curricula are likely to show little effect on knowledge and clinical skills. *Medical Education* 34, 729–738.

Anderson and Glew, R. H. (2002). Support of a problem-based learning curriculum by basic science faculty. MedOnline 7:10 (http://www.med-ed-online.org).

Blake, R. L., Hosokawa, M. C. and Riley S. L. (2000). Student performances on step 1 and 1 of the United States medical licensing examination following implementation of a problem-based learning curriculum. *Academic Medicine* January 75:1.

Kwan, C. Y. (2000). What is problem-based learning (PBL)? It is magic, myth and mindset. *Center for Development of Teaching and Learning*, August 3 (3)1–6.

Sweet, G. (1989). *The Advantage of Being Useless.* Pamerston Nor., New Zealand: The Bunmore Press, p. 6.

1

The Baby Boomers: The Story of the Johnsons

Mindfulness helps me to recognize what is happening in the present moment, and it also helps me to be aware when something is pulling me and taking away my stability and freedom. Sometimes I shun and sometimes I grasp at what is happening in the present moment. Both paths cause me to lose myself.

Thich Nhat Hanh

Getting Started

> "I'm so anxious I can hardly catch my breath every time I hear my co-workers talk about their children. One of my co-workers is pregnant and I cannot even look at her without crying. I'm spinning out of control."

What feelings and thoughts are you aware of right now?

_____

_____

Sharon is forty-seven years old and married to Jonathan, who is forty-nine years old. They are African American and have been married for seventeen years. Sharon was self-referred to the community counseling center. She came to the first session with Jonathan. Sharon is timid and indecisive and often has difficulty expressing her feelings and opinions because she fears rejection. Jonathan is outgoing and suffered a serious spinal injury in college playing football; he walks with a cane and often needs the assistance of a wheelchair. Sharon has been unable to tell Jonathan about her anxiety at work.

Sharon speaks rapidly, with one sentence running into the next, and often loses her train of thought. She comes to the initial session concerned about her mind racing, her feelings of anxiety, and her tendency to cry for no apparent reason. Sharon and Jonathan have no children, although they state they like children and wanted to start a family but kept putting off making the commitment. Jonathan is an assertive and decisive man. He is confused about Sharon's symptoms.

- What do you know about panic attacks?

_____

_____

- How would you deal with Sharon's anxiety?

_____

_____

- What relaxation techniques might you suggest for Sharon?

_____

_____

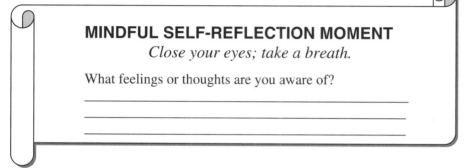

MINDFUL SELF-REFLECTION MOMENT

Close your eyes; take a breath.

What feelings or thoughts are you aware of?

_____

_____

_____

A Window into the Past

Sharon

Sharon is a petite and delicate woman and the older of two children born to Joanna and Will. Sharon and her sibling were raised in a rural southeastern town in the United States and did not have a large extended family living nearby. Most of Sharon's relatives lived in the city several miles away. Joanna and Will moved to a small rural community when they married. They attended a local Baptist church, and Sharon describes the members of community church like family. Sharon describes herself growing up as a "good girl" who wanted to please her parents. Both parents were artists, Joanna a painter and Will a wood carver. Sharon was born with an operatic voice, yet she was extremely shy and soft-spoken when she was not singing. Her younger brother Darell was rebellious and created chaos in the home. Much attention was given to Darell. Sharon reported that she "melted into the background" unnoticed and spent much time alone. She had an opportunity to pursue a career as an opera singer (she received a full college scholarship), but her shyness prevented her from pursuing her dream. Several years later she left home to attend a local college, where she met Jonathan.

How might Sharon's experiences as a child have impacted her life as an adult?

_____

_____

Jonathan

Jonathan is a strong and handsome man and the second oldest of four boys born to Harold and Mary. Jonathan was raised in a large extended family and remembers visiting and growing up in frequent contact with his cousins, aunts, and uncles. His maternal and paternal grandparents lived nearby and often visited and helped with the children. Jonathan was raised in a large southeastern city. He describes his childhood home as lively, with relatives and friends coming and going. His mother loved animals; hence, there were usually several dogs and cats living among the large family. Jonathan excelled in sports and was a high school football star. He enjoyed the attention and excitement of those earlier years. He played college football for one year until he incurred a spinal injury. Jonathan was fortunate to survive; yet he has difficulty walking without a cane and needs a wheelchair for distance maneuvering. He met Sharon in college and immediately knew "she was the woman of his dreams."

- What emotional changes might Jonathan have experienced as a result of his accident?

  _____

  _____

- What questions might you formulate based on the Johnson's story?

  _____

  _____

Sharon and Jonathan

Sharon and Jonathan enjoyed many years exploring the outdoors and being in nature. They put off starting a family because they wanted to enjoy their independence and freedom. Both Sharon and Jonathan's parents hoped they would have grandchildren and were disappointed about their putting off starting a family. Jonathan's brothers all had children and often teased him about not having children. Sharon and Jonathan built a small house and loved their dog and cat, but they often felt the longing for the laughter of children in their home. Jonathan liked his work as an engineer, but Sharon was never able to find her niche. Although she was a gifted singer and had creative talents, her fears and anxiety prevented her from pursuing a career in the arts. Instead she settled for an office position that she excelled in but that did not nurture her creative talents.

Although Jonathan was a confident and opinionated man who felt deeply for Sharon, his limited mobility added to Sharon's responsibility. Jonathan expressed his interest in Sharon and her ideas, yet Sharon felt controlled by him due to her inability to express herself with conviction. She would rather settle for Jonathan's plans than risk a disagreement. As a result, Sharon began harboring deep resentments toward Jonathan, which manifested in sudden outbursts and, more recently, frequent episodes of rapid heart rate, shortness of breath, and mind racing.

- What issues might you address at this point?

_____

_____

- How might you approach Sharon about her lack of confidence?

_____

_____

- What clinical interventions might you explore with Sharon and Jonathan?

_____

_____

MINDFUL SELF-REFLECTION MOMENT
Close your eyes; take a breath.

What feelings or thoughts are you aware of?

_____

_____

_____

Embracing the Essence

Following years of delayed family planning, Sharon became obsessed with her desire for a child. She was so anxious when thinking about it that she could hardly breathe and was unable to concentrate on the smallest task. She became isolated at work, eating lunch alone and unable to have conversations with her co-workers because she feared "mothers talking about their children." One day while Sharon was shopping for clothes, she felt short of breath and fainted in the store. She was admitted to the emergency room and was unable to explain what happened.

Due to her age, Sharon discussed with Jonathan the option of adoption, and he did not want to take that chance. He worried about the unknown problems that an adopted child may come with. Sharon and Jonathan decided to interview with a fertilization specialist. They decide to use a donor egg and Jonathan's sperm. Due to Sharon's age, they needed to act immediately for safety and eligibility. Sharon found out two months later that she was pregnant with twin boys.

- What questions might you ask of Sharon and Jonathan at this point?

  _____

  _____

- What are your thoughts about Sharon's pregnancy?

  _____

  _____

- What issues might Sharon and Jonathan fear as older parents, particularly given Jonathan's disability?

  _____

  _____

THOUGHTS TO PONDER

Passive breathing, slow breaths through the lips, is an excellent intervention for hyperventilation syndrome. A hyperventilating client simply breathes too rapidly and deeply under stress, and as a result, exhales too much carbon dioxide. This can trigger a variety of symptoms (cramping in the abdomen, dizziness, fatigue, hot flashes, loss of consciousness, panic, pains in chest, rapidly beating heart, nausea, tension trembling), which may be misinterpreted by the client as anxiety or panic. (Smith, 2005, p. 115)

TAKE A ONE-MINUTE VACATION

To fully experience the stretch, start each energy exercise slowly, deepen your breathing, release the breath (letting go of any sounds that may arise), stay relaxed and loose, and slowly pick up the pace. On the exhale, let the sound of **HA** become increasingly strong. The **HA** sound is a forceful exhaling release. Allow yourself to let the sound go free as it happens. These stretches are energizing and invigorating!

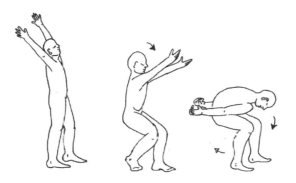

Brushing Floor Stand with feet comfortably apart, and swing your arms forward and back. Keep your knees slightly bent, press your feet into the ground, and exhale **HA** as you bend forward and brush floor with fingertips. Inhale, and return to standing as you swing your arms up over your head and repeat. Lightly bounce your knees and ankles as your arms swing down and again as your arms swing up.

Exploratory Research and Resource Corner

- What homework assignments might you explore to help Sharon and Jonathan?

_____

_____

- Describe relevant resources that might help in working with the Johnsons.

_____

_____

Celebrating Family Culture

Jonathan and Sharon Johnson were both raised in the southeastern United States. Their detained desire to have children put them at risk due to Sharon's age. In addition, Jonathan's disability undoubtedly posed a problem because of his limited physical ability. Being raised in the southeastern United States presented other issues for this African American couple; in the Southeast, familial, religious, and social values impacted their lives. Although they live in a predominately African American community; they are both minority professionals in their place of business.

Research has shown that African American men born and raised in the South were more traditional than European American men in terms of self-reliance, achievement/status, attitudes toward sexuality, and restrictive emotionality. These findings offer insight into the significance African American men place on being the provider and caretaker for their families and the gender role of being strong (Levant, Majors, & Kelley, 1998, pp. 233–234). Jonathan's physical disability posed a constant challenge in raising twin boys. Jonathan is faced with potential discrimination on several levels: being an African American man, having a physical disability, and being an older parent of young children. He struggles to be productive and active in assuming the role of strength for his family.

There are several issues to be considered for Jonathan and others with disabilities who face discrimination. The prevalence in language used to separate people with disabilities stands out; for example, separate buses, separate entrances, separate drinking fountains, separate bathrooms, and separate classrooms. "Much like the signs of yesteryear reading 'White' and 'Colored,' today there are signs designating separate entrances for people with disabilities" (Olkin, 2002, p. 134). People with physical disabilities are generally the only one in the family and sometimes even their community to have a particular disability.

People with disabilities are different from other groups vulnerable to discrimination because they often experience pain, fatigue, and muscle weakness. These challenges often require hired help, assistive technology, and adapted equipment, all of which impact financial resources. In addition, the high unemployment rate of 66 percent for people with disabilities can make these accommodations unaffordable. For Jonathan, an African American man, his role and status in the family as provider and protector can be threatened and impair his self-image, which can cause stress.

The extended family is an important system for the Johnsons. The extended family in African-American families often includes the church community and neighbors as well as parents, siblings, and other relatives. The family network is inclusive and interdependent, offering various opportunities for support.

Most of Sharon's relatives had their children at a young age. Sharon's children are the age of her contemporaries' grandchildren. Research has shown that women over age forty have a high rate of miscarriage (Nybo, Wohlfahrt, Christens Olsen, & Melbye, 2000, p. 1708). Due to Jonathan's disability, Sharon needs to work full time, which can add to her existing anxiety disorder. Seeking out suitable daycare for the boys will also be a challenge. Sharon needs to care for Jonathan because he has many physical limitations. The threat of unemployment for Jonathan is ever constant as he has been discriminated against in several places of employment and was forced out of one job several years ago. In a study comparing African American and European American women's marital well-being, physical health (individual) and in-law relations (social and economic) affected the marital well-being of only African American women (Goodwin, 2003, p. 550).

Both Jonathan and Sharon will have the additional challenge of raising twin boys. Although twins have many commonalities, they also have different personalities, and interests and often develop physically, emotionally, and intellectually at different rates which often presents a challenge to parents of multiple birth children. In addition, Sharon is approaching menopause, which may be accelerated due to the hormonal changes associated with the pregnancy. She is beginning to experience "hot flashes" and often has trouble sleeping. Both Jonathan and Sharon are first-time parents, and adjusting to the changes in the relationship—particularly Sharon's availability to help Jonathan physically while sharing the responsibility of household chores and parenting—can be a challenge.

- How might the cultural norms and the issues of oppression impact the lives of the Johnsons?

_____

_____

- What strengths of the Johnsons are you aware of?

_____

_____

MINDFUL SELF-REFLECTION MOMENT
Close your eyes; take a breath.

What feelings or thoughts are you aware of?

_____

_____

_____

THERAPIST'S TOOLS

When working with couples, an important tool is to "listen"
to the interactions of the couple. This includes what is said,
tones of voice, how the body responds to what is being said,
and how the couple uses language. Being able to focus on the
moment-to-moment interaction without getting caught up in the drama of the story
will help you as the therapist to observe the unconscious process and dynamics.
How can we move deeper into the unconscious process with Sharon and Jonathan?

1. *Work with defenses.* Support their defenses and 'go with the resistance' to facilitate empathy.
2. *Be creative.* Ask Sharon and Jonathan to step into each other's shoes and demon-
   strate voice tone, body language, and behavior by a role reversal that allows
   each partner to take the role of the other.
3. *Create safe emergencies.* Create situations in the session for Jonathan and Sharon
   to explore how they feel about each other in ways that are new and novel. The
   therapist offers a suggestion of enactment using a gestalt therapy 'empty chair'
   model. Sharon and Jonathan take turns reflecting, confronting and exploring
   feelings toward each other using the empty chair eliciting feelings that are new
   and challenging (Moursund and Erskine, 2004, p. 169).

Riding the Wave

Both Jonathan and Sharon were thrilled with the news of having twin boys, yet Sharon's feelings of inadequacy began to rear its head. "I haven't been around children in years," Sharon said.

- How would you support Sharon and Jonathan at this point?

  _____

  _____

- How might an experiential therapist work with the Johnsons?

  _____

  _____

- What clinical interventions might you consider at this point in treatment?

  _____

  _____

- What are some issues that may arise for the twins having older parents?

  _____

  _____

Session with Sharon, Jonathan, and Therapist

THERAPIST: Congratulations to you both. How are you feeling?

SHARON: Great, we're so happy. (She then begins talking rapidly about incidentals at work and the home.)

THERAPIST: It seems to me like you're having a difficult time focusing today.

SHARON: Well, yes, since the pregnancy I have not been taking any anxiety medication, OK, but, I feel OK, but, yes, sometimes I go off on a tangent and forget where I started.

JONATHAN: Sometimes she drives me crazy. She talks on and on about stuff and I don't even know what we're talking about after a while.

THERAPIST: I hear your frustration: let's try to help Sharon stay on track. (Therapist turns to Sharon.) Sharon, can we try a relaxation exercise to help you focus today?

SHARON: OK, I'll try anything. I'm feeling a bit out of control, my mind is racing.

THERAPIST: Close your eyes, listen only to the sounds of your breath, very slowly, breathing in and out. Give yourself a few minutes to let go, relax.

SHARON: (Begins and calms down. Facial muscles are relaxed.)

THERAPIST: Sharon, with gentle intention, focus inward and let yourself become aware of what you are experiencing right now.

SHARON: I'm feeling confused, happy about the pregnancy and being a mom yet scared of both. I feel my heart beating fast like it's going to jump out of my body. My legs ache.

JONATHAN: I feel happy and a bit scared, too.

SHARON: Maybe you do understand what I'm feeling. I think I can share with you without feeling so anxious.

What are your thoughts about the session with Sharon and Jonathan?

_____

_____

Exploratory Research and Resource Corner

• What resources would help you in working with Sharon?

_____

_____

• What literature would you explore in your research to gain more knowledge in treating Jonathan and Sharon?

_____

_____

• What homework assignments might you explore with the Johnsons?

_____

_____

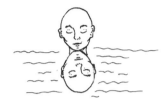

MINDFUL SELF-REFLECTION MOMENT
Close your eyes; take a breath.

What feelings or thoughts are you aware of?

_____

_____

_____

THOUGHTS TO PONDER

Years ago, Bandler, a psychologist, and Grinder, a linguist, combined their efforts to create and teach the theory and application of changing our mental language. They called it neurolinguistic programming (NLP). Neurolinguistic programming is designed to look at how our thoughts control our language and how our language influences our behavior. (Seaward, 2004, p. 205) Neurolinguistic programming is an empowering skill to reprogram the software of human linguistics so that our human energies can be focused in the direction of our highest human potential or human excellence. Part selective awareness, part self-hypnosis, the dynamics of NLP work to eliminate the self defeating thoughts that inhibit our energies and keep us from reaching our goals. (Seaward, 2004, p. 192)

Beyond Treatment

Sharon returned to work six weeks after the boys were born. She loved being with the babies, yet she continued to feel overwhelmed because her responsibilities did not decrease—she had to take care of the babies and the home while still assisting Jonathan. Most of the time she was exhausted and exhilarated simultaneously. In addition, she was experiencing hormonal changes due to the pregnancy and early menopause. Jonathan was delighted to be a father. He wanted to help as much as physically possible, yet Sharon was nervous that he might drop a baby or trip and fall. This was an area of continual negotiation for them. The family was excited about the twins and spent time visiting and helping on weekends. Sharon welcomed the help, yet usually she felt a need to make everyone comfortable by cooking and being a welcoming hostess. It was difficult for her to ask for help, yet she enjoyed it when it came. At times she wished she did not have to work full time, yet she wondered what it would be like to have the boys at home alone full time. Sharon and Jonathan felt a renewed spirit that stemmed from being parents and sharing the daily nuances and changes with the boys.

Describe how you would prepare the Johnsons for termination of counseling.

REFERENCES

Goodwin, P. Y. (2003). African American and European American Women's marital well-being. *Journal of Marriage and Family, 65*(3), 550–560.

Hanh, T. N. (2004). *Touching the earth—intimate conversations with the Buddha.* Berkeley, CA: Parallax Press.

Levant, R. F., Majors, R. G., & Kelley, M. L. (1998). Masculinity ideology among young African American and European American women and men in different regions of the United States. *Cultural Diversity and Ethnic Minority Psychology, 4*(3), 227–236.

Moursund, J. P. & Erskine, R. G. (2004). *Integrative psychotherapy: The art and science of relationship.* Thomson: Brooks/Cole.

Napoli, M. (2000). Successful integrative counseling techniques: Ancient tools for modern treatment. *Arizona Counseling Journal, 22*(1), 15–24.

Nichols, M. P. & Schwartz, R. C. (2006). *Family therapy: Concepts and methods.* Pearson/Allyn and Bacon, Boston.

Nybo, A. M., Wohlfahrt, J., Christens, P., Olsen, J., & Melbye, M. (2000). Maternal age and fetal loss: Population based register linkage study. *British Medical Journal, 320*(7251), 1708–1712.

Olkin, R. (2002). Could you hold the door for me? Including disability in diversity. *Cultural Diversity and Ethnic Minority Psychology, 8*(2), 130–137.

Protinsky, H., Flemke, K., & Sparks, J. (2001). EMDR and emotionally oriented couples therapy. *Contemporary Family Therapy, 23*(2), 153–168.

Seward, B. L. (2006). *Managing stress: Principles and strategies for health and well being.* Sudbury, MA: Jones and Bartlett Publishers, Inc.

Smith, J. C. (2005). *Relaxation, meditation, and mindfulness: A mental health practitioner's guide to new and traditional approaches.* New York: Springer Publishing.

SUGGESTED READINGS

Allen, W. D., & Olson, D. H. (2001). Five types of African-American marriages. *Journal of Marital and Family Therapy, 27*(3), 301–314.

Blank, M. B., Mahmood, M., Fox, J. C., & Guterbock, T. (2002). Alternative mental health services: The role of the black church in the south. *American Journal of Public Health, 92*(10), 1669–1672.

Brodkin, A. M. (1997). Twins, together too much? *Scholastic Early Childhood Today, 12*(3), 25–27.

Huppert, J. K., Schultz, L. T., Foa, E. B., Barlow, D. H., Davidson, J. R. T., Gorman, J. M., Shear, M. K., Simpson, H. B., & Woods, S. C. (2002). Differential response to placebo among patients with social phobia panic disorder and obsessive-compulsive disorder. *American Journal of Psychiatry, 161,* 1485–1487.

Matthews, A. K., Hughes, T. L. (2001). Mental health service use by African American women: Exploration of subpopulation differences. *Cultural Diversity and Ethnic Minority Psychology, 7*(1), 75–87.

Moilanen, I., Linna, S. L., Ebeling, H., Kumpulainenk, K., Tamminen, T., Piha, J., & Amqvist, F. (1999). Are twins' behavioural emotional problems different from singletons'? *European Child and Adolescent Psychiatry, 8*(4), 62–70.

Spence, W. D., Kayumov, L., Chen, A., Lowe, A., Jain, U., Katzman, M. A., Shen, J., Perelman, B., & Shapiro, C. (2004). Acupuncture increases nocturnal melatonin secretion and reduces insomnia and anxiety: A preliminary report. *The Journal of Neurophisiatry and Clinical Neurosciences, 16,* 19–28.

2

The Reluctant Divorce: The Story of the Wilsons

Wisdom tells me I am nothing. Love tells me I am everything.
And between the two my life flows.
Nisargfadatta Maharj, in Levey & Levey, 1998, p. 132

Getting Started

"Could I have been this blind? My husband Jason molested my two daughters and slept with every woman he could find. I feel so ashamed to walk down the road and face the community. Everyone knows but me!"

What reactions are you aware of right now?

_____

_____

Phyllis is a thirty-five-year-old Native Navajo woman who was self-referred to the tribal social services. She reported that she has been living with her husband Jason for seven years. She has one daughter from a prior relationship, Rachel, who is thirteen years old, and three daughters, eight-year-old twins and a ten-month-old, from her relationship with Jason. Phyllis knew that Jason drank too much and sometimes didn't come home, but she turned a blind eye to this behavior. Recently, Phyllis became aware during a parent-teacher conference at Rachel's school that Jason was molesting Rachel.

- Describe your thoughts about why Phyllis might turn a blind eye toward Jason's behavior.

_____

_____

- What do you know about children who have been sexually abused?

_____

_____

- What clinical techniques would help you during this initial phase of treatment?

_____

_____

THOUGHTS TO PONDER

"To prevent Post Traumatic Stress Disorder in sexually abused women, self esteem support is critical. If the victims perceive that others value them it may help counteract self blame." (Hymann, Gold, & Cott, 2003, p. 298)

Family session with Phyllis, Jason, Rachel, twins Cora and Janelle, and social service counselor, who is an elderly Native American man respected in the community. Session took place at the Tribal Social Service Office.

Note: The therapist used circular communication here. This type of communication is often used in Indigenous cultures where casual 'small talk' or sharing a story precedes discussion of the task at hand. This circular communication set the stage to let the client feel connected to the therapist. There is often a lesson being communicated through metaphor.

THERAPIST: Good morning, I'm happy to see that all of you can make it today. (Therapist spends about twenty minutes discussing a community activity that took place the previous weekend. He also shares a story about a visit from a relative who stole some money from his grandmother and had unfortunate luck after the incident. He notes that his relative felt shame about the incident, turned his life around, and began a community project for youth of making native crafts.)

PHYLLIS: (Says the girls enjoyed the event and nods her head in acknowledgment about the therapist's story and thanks the therapist for making time for her family.)

JASON: I don't know why I'm here. She (looking at Phyllis) doesn't know how to raise our daughters. I was raised in a traditional family and I don't like that our girls are going to the town school getting crazy ideas about the "white man's world."

THERAPIST: (Therapist speaks softly and leans forward, facing Jason.) I would like to hear more about your concerns, Jason.

JASON: You know, you're a Native man, you need to keep these women in line, otherwise they stray from home.

PHYLLIS: If it weren't for the school, we would not have known what's been happening with Rachel and you.

THERAPIST: (Looks at Rachel; she hunches over and covers her face; therapist moves his chair closer to Rachel and speaks softly.) Can you tell us what you are feeling right now? Take a moment.

RACHEL: (Peeks up at Jason, fear in her eyes.)

THERAPIST: I wonder if it would be more comfortable if you and I met for a few minutes alone.

RACHEL: (Shrugs her shoulders, nods her head, yes.)

THERAPIST: (To Jason, Phyllis, and the children.) We have some drinks and fruit in the kitchen; maybe you can help yourself and the children to some snacks for a few minutes while Rachel and I meet.

- What are your thoughts about how the therapist began the session?

  _____

  _____

- How might you deal with Rachel?

  _____

  _____

- Would you have done anything different in the session? If so, describe.

  _____

  _____

Therapist and Rachel meet alone in another room.

THERAPIST: (Sits across from Rachel at a comfortable distance but close enough to make contact.) I thought it would be more comfortable for us to meet alone since it seems to me that you were uncomfortable with your dad in the room.

RACHEL: (Jaw tightens, voice constrained.) He's not my dad.

THERAPIST: I see, he's your step dad.

RACHEL: Yeah, I hate him!

THERAPIST: Rachel, can you take a moment, breathe slowly. What thoughts or feelings are you aware of? Notice any feelings or sensations in your body.

RACHEL: (Sits for a few minutes and tears begin to flow.)

THERAPIST: It's OK to experience your feelings, Rachel; I'm here; can you put those feelings into words?

RACHEL: When he looks at me I feel disgusting.

THERAPIST: Can you tell me more about feeling disgusting?

RACHEL: He comes into my room at night and touches me. (Tears still flowing.)

THERAPIST: It must have been hard for you to keep this a secret; I can see how badly you feel about what happened.

RACHEL: (Nods her head yes.) I can't go back in there with him.

THERAPIST: Would you mind if I go in and meet with your family?

RACHEL: OK; I don't know how you can help.

THERAPIST: We will find a way to protect you.

(Therapist offers Rachel to sit with the child protective counselor and offers her a drink and some snacks.)

Therapist enters room to talk with Phyllis, Jason, Cora, and Janelle.

THERAPIST: (Breaks the ice.) Have you had your snacks? (Everyone nods.) Rachel will not be joining us for the rest of the session. She feels uncomfortable about some things that have been happening. (Turning to face Jason.)

JASON: You know how teenagers are, they want their way and she doesn't like to be disciplined.

CORA: (Looks at therapist.) I know why she's uncomfortable; she doesn't like Dad touching her. I don't like it either; he touches me when I'm sleeping.

PHYLLIS: (Looks shocked and starts to cry.)

JASON: That's crazy. I don't know why the girls are trying to make trouble for me. Maybe they want attention and think this is the way to get what they want.

THERAPIST: Jason, maybe you and I can meet together for a while alone. (Turns to Phyllis, Cora, and Janelle.) Can you join Rachel in the other room while dad and I talk?

- Where might the therapist be going with the Wilsons?

  _____

  _____

- What might Phyllis be experiencing right now?

  _____

  _____

- Describe your thoughts and reaction to Jason's behavior in this session.

  _____

  _____

- What more do you need to know?

_____

_____

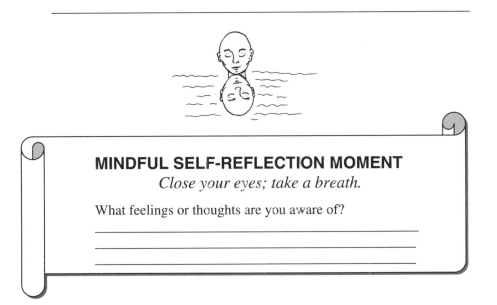

MINDFUL SELF-REFLECTION MOMENT

Close your eyes; take a breath.

What feelings or thoughts are you aware of?

_____

_____

_____

A Window into the Past

Jason

Jason is a tense thirty-eight-year-old Navajo man who was born and raised on a small rural reservation in the southwest United States. He has been gainfully employed most of his life working as a long-haul truck driver. His father died tragically in an automobile accident when Jason was eight years old. After his father's death, his mother became involved with alcohol consumption and became an unstable figure who drifted in and out of Jason's life. Jason was raised by his paternal grandparents, aunts, and uncles, in a large, extended traditional and prominent family of livestock traders on his reservation. He married Phyllis, a Navajo woman from another clan, ten years ago. They have lived on his reservation with their children near his family.

Phyllis

Phyllis is a quiet thirty-five-year-old Navajo woman who was born and raised on a small reservation in the southwest United States. She was the oldest daughter of five girls and raised in a traditional Navajo family. Her father was a sheep herder and she attended a tribal school on the reservation. She was raised with her maternal and paternal aunts, uncles, and cousins. Her father was a known philanderer in her home of origin. She married Darrell when she was twenty-five years old and had Rachel. She divorced Darrell, who was emotionally abusive. Phyllis's mother suffered from depression and was hospitalized several times during Phyllis's growing years. The family felt that Phyllis's mother was like her great grandmother and carrying a "bad spirit," and family members often avoided her.

- How might the death of Jason's father and abandonment of his mother impact his relationship with Phyllis?

  _____

  _____

- Although Phyllis and Jason are from the same tribe, how might the difference in clans impact their family life?

  _____

  _____

Jason and Phyllis

Phyllis was initially very happy when she met Jason. He seemed strong and confident, and she thought that he would be an adequate provider because his family had a large livestock trade. He was accepting of her daughter Rachel, and Phyllis felt that he would be a good father to her; Rachel had been a victim of emotional abuse at the hands of Phyllis's former husband, Darrell. They lived in Jason's house on his reservation in the Southwest. Phyllis tried to visit her family, but the distance was great and she did not like to travel alone. Jason was not interested in visiting her family. Several times during the year, Phyllis's sisters would visit, and these visits were important to Phyllis because they gave her a sense of connection to her family.

Jason had several on-and-off-again affairs with various women in the small community in which he and Phyllis and Rachel lived. Phyllis avoided the gossip and felt deeply ashamed that she had these problems in her marriage. She would rationalize that Jason's behavior was normal for most men, that he really loved her and would stop if she just could love him more. The final blow came when Jason was found to have been molesting Rachel and Cora. Jason's drinking worsened and he was becoming more agitated toward family members. Jason denied having an alcohol problem; he stated that he was a good provider and that the family should be grateful for having a roof over their heads. Phyllis and the girls kept their distance. Jason was out one evening, drinking heavily and driving. He ran a red light and caused an accident. He injured a small child and the child's father. Jason passed out behind the wheel.

- What factors may have contributed to Jason's alcoholism?

  _____

  _____

- What might Phyllis do to feel more connected to her family?

  _____

  _____

Embracing the Essence

Phyllis made the decision that her marriage was not as important as her children's safety. When she confronted Jason with her new-found information, Jason became enraged and accused Rachel and Cora of lying and trying to "come on" to him. Jason threatened to have Phyllis and Rachel evicted from their home and to gain custody of their three younger daughters. Phyllis knew that the dynamics and laws of the tribe would most likely favor the husband, who was an enrolled tribal member. Her ambivalence in this situation was greatly magnified. She was fearful of leaving her husband and second marriage, as well as reluctant to subject her children to growing up without their father. Phyllis was afraid of what would happen to Jason due to being arrested for driving under the influence, injuring two community members, and having to face the charges of sexual molestation. The community was talking about the incident, and Phyllis found out about several women with whom Jason was involved.

- What factors may contribute to Phyllis' ambivalence?

  _____

  _____

- What do you need to know about the treatment of trauma?

  _____

  _____

- What are your thoughts about Jason's recent incident?

  _____

  _____

TAKE A ONE-MINUTE VACATION

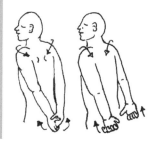

Shoulder Squeeze Fingers behind back, press hands away from shoulders, lengthening arms. Allow chest to open as shoulder blades squeeze together. Squeeze buttocks and tuck tail bone under gently.

Exploratory Research and Resource Corner

- What resources and/or literature would be helpful for you to explore now?

_____

_____

- What tasks or homework assignments can you explore with Phyllis and her daughters to help them feel more secure at this time?

_____

_____

Jason was arrested by the FBI and eventually housed off the reservation in an undisclosed location as his case went through court. He was given a term in jail and probation. When he was released he was admitted to a rehabilitation center for alcohol and sexual addiction. Jason had been ordered to complete a sixty-day program of inpatient treatment. He had been initially exhibiting some behaviors and making comments indicating that he felt he was "better than many of the others there" and was argumentative and aloof. In the initial two weeks of his stay, he had basically alienated the other residents—fifteen other men ranging from eighteen to fifty-two years old—with his condescending and disparaging remarks. Jason confided in his primary counselor that since he had remained consistently employed from a young age, he felt that he was a stable father figure to his children, that he had more "on the ball" than the rest of "these losers." He was truly an unpleasant person to be around in early substance abstinence.

The therapeutic goals of inpatient treatment are to (1) help the chemically dependent person remain abstinent from the substance of choice (in Jason's case, alcohol); (2) develop peer support in coping with the resurfacing feelings, including, anger, fear, sadness, and shame (in Jason's case, his feelings about sexually abusing his daughters, having extramarital affairs, and injuring the boy and his father in the automobile accident); and (2) gain insight into patterns of use and abuse of chemicals through a series of readings and written assignments; and (4) make some healthy contacts that will support him in a sober way. The only goal that Jason was able to grasp was by default, the ability to remain abstinent from alcohol, because he was in an environment where alcohol was not readily available. However, instead of processing his feelings of shame, fear, loss of control, and uncertainty, he chose to deny and sublimate the strong feelings that he carried so they came out in ways that irritated and estranged others. Jason refused to perform any of the written assignments or readings and chose to sit, scowling, with his arms folded in meetings, and to draw pictures during his free time.

What might be going on with Jason? How would you deal with his behavior?

_____

_____

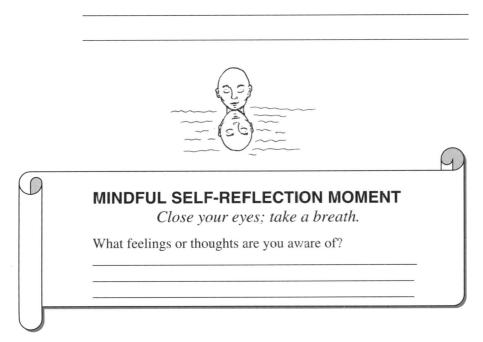

MINDFUL SELF-REFLECTION MOMENT
Close your eyes; take a breath.

What feelings or thoughts are you aware of?

_____

_____

_____

Extended family session.

The staff at the rehabilitation center decided to ask Jason if he would like to have a session with his family. Jason's two older uncles, an aunt, nieces and nephews, cousins, and his grandmother drove four hours just to be with him and have the opportunity to talk with him. A total of thirteen people were gathered in the counselor's small office one morning, each pouring out his or her heart and touting the merits of a sober lifestyle to Jason. They expressed their feelings and were happy to finally have him sober so they could present their concerns to him. Jason's grandmother talked for nearly an hour, in her Native tongue, and Jason began to weep as she spoke. She told him of her love for him, that he did not have to be afraid anymore, that she felt proud of her family, and that she had hopeful expectations of him. In addition, she shared many other jewels of wisdom. Each family member, including some very restless children, were given the opportunity to share verbally with Jason, and in the three-hour session, some wonderful thoughts were exchanged.

- What are your thoughts about the extended family session?

  _____

  _____

- Describe what happened to Jason in the session.

  _____

  _____

- What are your thoughts about how a traditional healer or ceremony might support Jason?

  _____

THOUGHTS TO PONDER

Following residential rehabilitation for addiction, to ensure sobriety it is crucial to

1. Maintain a support system through family, self-help, friends, and therapy.
2. Find alternative, empowering activities to prevent addictive behavior.
3. Develop a spiritual practice to maintain harmony.

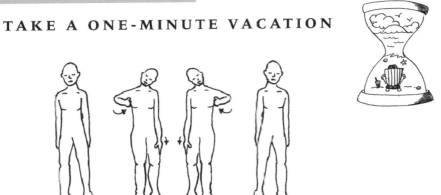

TAKE A ONE-MINUTE VACATION

Monkey Stand with feet slightly wider than shoulder width apart, bend knees a bit, and relax arms at side. Press soles of feet into the ground, squeeze the buttocks, and exhale "ha!" making fist with left hand and sliding it into the left armpit while your right hand slides down the right leg. Allow torso to bend to the right and lean into the right leg for support. Inhale, return to center, and repeat on other side several times, going side to side.

Celebrating Family Culture

The Wilson family illustrates common dilemmas among First Nations Peoples. When we trace the historical roots, we see a people invested not only in the individual and family, but equally invested in the community in which they live. One's identity is formed by the tribe, which offers structure, meaning, purpose, and a sense of belonging. The devastating results of colonization, in which millions were murdered, land was stolen, and traditions and language were eliminated have seriously impacted the self-perceptions of First Nations Peoples. The effects of poverty have further impacted the survival of First Nations Peoples.

First Nations men have been subjugated; as a result they often have turned against their children and partners, particularly with the high incidence of alcohol abuse. Krech (2002) discusses the importance of men's role in their communities, each having a specific function in the perpetuation of cultural norms and practices. "Survival for Indigenous men during the establishment of encroaching nations has often occurred through relinquishment of a part of 'self' psychically. Aboriginal men report experiencing hopelessness, living in a self-imposed isolation, even through a sense of tradition or direction" (p. 77). Jason struggled with his poor self-esteem and with maintaining respect for his family and traditional values.

Native women and men have suffered high rates of trauma, either witnessed or experienced, often related to physical attacks and other forms of violence (Manson, Beals, Klein, Croy, & AI-SUPERPFP team, 2005). As a result of continued exposure to violence and trauma, Native men and women have high rates of Post Traumatic Stress Disorder. A study of PTSD in a Southwestern American Indian community found that "the most predictive factor for lifetime PTSD among women was the experience of physical assault and the prevalence of lifetime PTSD and of exposure to a traumatic event were higher than in the general population of the United States (Robin, Chester, Rasmussen, Jaranson, & Goldman, 1997, p. 1582). Through the years Native women have been supported by each other while working together in groups, cooking, caring for children, sewing, gardening, and other activities that brought them together. The onset of colonization and industrialization has left women with more responsibility and less support, thus increasing isolation, illness, poverty and abuse (Napoli, 2000).

Guidelines for non-Native clinicians working with First Nations Peoples.

1. *Trust:* Acceptance by the non-Native therapist of the differences in values and traditions and the willingness of the non-Native therapist to self-disclose with sensitivity will facilitate trust in the client-therapist relationship.

2. *Spirituality:* Non-Native therapists need to acknowledge the significance of various spiritual beliefs, the role of the traditional healer, and Native people's connection with the spiritual world.

3. *Time:* Non-Native therapists need to let go of rigid scheduling, time constraints, and overplanning and allow for spontaneity.

4. *Communication:* Non-Native therapists need to understand the importance of silence, possible lack of eye contact, circular conversation, storytelling, and humor so that there is congruence in the interaction between client and therapist.

5. *Individual versus the family and community:* Non-Native therapists need to understand how the family and community play a major role in the client's identity, sense of responsibility, and life in general. This supersedes Western clinical ideology of the individual and individuation from one's family of origin (Napoli, 1999).

Jason and Phyllis were both raised in traditional Navajo families. Jason's drinking, infidelity, and sexual abuse toward his daughters set him apart from his traditional values and created distance between himself and his family.

THERAPIST'S TOOLS

*It is through the sacred that our lives become connected
to something deeper, richer, and more fulfiling.*
Kammen & Gold, 1998, p. 20

Creating ceremony in the treatment room can move clients toward transformation in unique ways. Ceremony does not necessarily need to be related to the family/client's religious beliefs; in fact, therapists can be creative in offering opportunities for ceremony related to just about every issue in which the family/client may be stuck or on which attention needs to be focused. As a therapist working with the Wilsons, the issues of betrayal, sexual abuse, and loss are paramount. Let's look at some possibilities.

Betrayal: Phyllis felt betrayed by Jason when he had affairs with other women. You might ask Phyllis to take an object, something simple such as a rock or a flower. Ask her to hold the object in her hand, close to her heart; breathe for a minute or two to allow the body to become aware of the feelings. Ask Phyllis to create an intention about what she wants to do with those feelings.

Sexual abuse: The trauma of sexual abuse often creates the feeling of numbness in the body. While sitting in a comfortable position, guide Rachel through a body scan after bringing awareness to each body part. Ask Rachel to say an empowering statement to herself, such as "You are loved," "You are special." This can begin creating a loving presence, a sense of self-acceptance and positive body awareness for Rachel.

Loss: Take Jason on a short nature walk; ask him to collect items in nature (twigs, rocks, leaves) and find a comfortable place to sit. Begin a guided imagery facilitating the memory of significant losses while Jason holds the objects. Each object is a representation of the loss. Ask Jason to make an offering of prayer or heartfelt words to his losses and return the objects to nature in a sacred space of his choice with the intention of letting them go.

Family vision: Bring Jason, Phyllis, Rachel, Cora, and Janelle together. Using a large posterboard, ask the family to bring in photos and magazines. Ask each family member to add to the poster. When the poster is complete, ask each family member to tell a story about his or her vision for the family, take the poster home, and display it in a place where everybody can see it daily. (Note that activities are appropriate only when therapist and clients agree and feel comfortable with the activities.)

Riding the Wave

Phyllis

The therapist helped Phyllis to obtain information about legal services and the extent of her rights as a nontribal member. Phyllis found that as the spouse of a tribal member (and mother of tribal children), she had certain rights and privileges that she had been unaware of. She was put in contact with legal services and referred to a clinician who specialized in issues relating to sexual abuse of children. Phyllis received help in finding financial resources for displaced homemakers. Both Rachel and Cora attended a group for sexually abused children, and Phyllis and her daughters continued to meet with the social services counselor weekly for family counseling.

Phyllis enrolled in and completed a training program in computer design and was eventually hired by a local company near her community. She and her children were able to negotiate the transition successfully, although the children are deeply disturbed by the fact that their father is no longer living with them. Phyllis reports that she is often lonely, yet she feels triumphant in that she was able to see her way through a very difficult transition.

THOUGHTS TO PONDER

"Addiction is a pathological, recurring relationship with any mood-altering event, experience, person, or thing that causes major life problems. The addiction isn't *because* of the substances, experience, person, or thing. It is the *relationship* with the substance or experience that goes awry. There's nothing wrong with banana cream pie, sex, or alcohol. The *relationship* with these is what becomes pathological. Most of us would choose to stop using something that causes problems. *Addiction is a process of decreasing choice.* The consequences of the use increase and the ability to make choices decreases. Addicts hang on to these problem producers." (Kellogg, 1990, p. 71)

Jason

Following the session with Jason's extended family.

After that morning, Jason seemed to become less tense, and he began to invest himself in his recovery; he began to work on the written assignments and to share some of his feelings in group with his peers. His peers noticed and commented on the positive change that had taken place within him, and how they felt he had much to offer and had a bright future ahead of him. Jason, too, was able to express his former fear of losing control, and he joined a group for sex offenders. He was able to talk about his shame of molesting his daughters, losing his father and mother, and ultimately losing his wife and children. He now felt that he was free to feel, and able to diffuse these emotional constraints. He also remarked that he felt like alcohol was no longer needed for him to cope with life and that he hoped to make amends with his wife and children.

- What steps does Jason need to take to prevent addiction relapse?

  _____

  _____

- What is your clinical impression of Phyllis at this point?

  _____

  _____

- What challenges might Cora and Rachel face in future intimate relationships?

  _____

  _____

MINDFUL SELF-REFLECTION MOMENT
Close your eyes; take a breath.

What feelings or thoughts are you aware of?

_____

_____

_____

Beyond Treatment

- Phyllis is volunteering with other women who are undergoing difficult transitory situations and trying to keep their families in order.

- Jason has started a men's support group in his community that focuses on traditional practices and activities and offers the men an opportunity to share stories, receive support when personal and family challenges arise, and develop alternatives to addictions.

- Rachel and Cora participated in the victims of sexual abuse group for one year. The Wilson family is working toward reunification.

- What other services are needed to support the Wilson family?

  _____

  _____

- Would you suggest any involvement with the extended family of either Phyllis or Jason? Describe.

  _____

  _____

- Describe the strengths inherent in the Wilson family that will support them through their recovery.

  _____

  _____

REFERENCES

Hyman, S. M., Gold, S. N., & Cott, M. A. (2003). Forms of social support that moderate PTSD in childhood sexual abuse survivors. *Journal of Family Violence, 18*(5).

Kammen, C. & Gold, J. (1998). A call for the living tribe. In *Call to connection: bringing sacred tribal values into modern life*. Salt Lake City, Utah: Commune-A-Key Publishing, 27–39.

Kellogg, T. (1990). *Broken toys broken dreams: Understanding & healing codependency, compulsive behaviors & family*. BRAT, Inc.

Levey, J., & Levey, M. (1998). *Living in balance: A dynamic approach for creating harmony and wholeness in a chaotic world*. Berkeley, CA: Conari Press.

Martin, E. J., Dossey, B. M., Keegan, L, & Guzzetta, C. (2000). Incest/child sexual abuse counseling. *Holistic nursing: A handbook for practice*. Gaithersburg, Maryland: Aspen Publishers, Inc., 777–789.

McCloskey, J. (1998). Three generations of Navajo women: Negotiating life course strategies in the Eastern Navajo Agency. *American Indian Culture and Research Journal, 22*(2), 103–129.

Napoli, M. (1999). The Non-Indian therapist working with the American Indian client: Transference and countertransference issues. *Psychoanalytic Social Work, 6*(1), 25–47.

Robin, R. W., Chester, B., Rasmussen, J. K., Jaranson, J. M. & Goldman, D. (1997) Prevalence and characteristics of trauma and posttraumatic stress disorder in a southwestern American Indian community. *American Journal of Psychiatry, 154*, 1582–1588.

SUGGESTED READING

Anderson, L. E., Weston, E. A., Doueck, H. J., & Krause, D. J. (2002). The child-centered social worker and the sexually abused child: Pathway to healing. *Social Work: Journal of the National Association of Social Workers, 47*(4), 368–378.

Carillo, R., & Tello, J. (1998). *Family violence and men of color,* New York: Springer.

Dossey, L. (1993). How to pray and what to pray for. In *Healing Words: The power of prayer and the practice of medicine,* San Francisco, CA: Harper Collins, 89–108.

Edmond, T., Sloan, L., & McCarty, D. (2004). Sexual abuse survivors' perceptions of the effectiveness of EMDR and eclectic therapy. *Research on Social Work Practice, 14*(4), 259–272.

El-Khoury, M. Y., Dutton, M. A., Goodman, L. A., Ebgke, L., Belamaric, R. J., & Murphy, M. (2004). Ethnic differences in battered women's formal help-seeking strategies: A Focus on health, mental health, and spirituality. *Cultural diversity and Ethnic Minority Psychology, 10*(4), 383–339.

Krech, P. (2002). Envisioning a healthy future: A re-becoming of Native American men. *Journal of Sociology and Social Welfare, 29*(1), 77–96.

Manson, S. P.; Beals, J.; Klein. S. A.; Croy, C.; and the AI-SUPERPFT team. (2005) Social epidemiology of trauma among two American Indian reservation populations. *American Journal of Public Health. 95* (5). 851–859.

Napoli, M. (2000). American Indian women in the 21st century: The yearn to be heard. *Journal of International and Community Social Welfare, 17*(1), 55–61.

Napoli, M. (2002). Holistic health care for Native women: An integrated model. *American Journal of Public Health, 92*(10), 6–8.

Napoli, M., & Santin-Gonzalez, E. (2001). Intensive home-based treatment and wellness services for American Indian families. *Families and Society, 82,* 315–324.

Rieckmann, T. R., Wadsworth, M. E., & Deyhle, D. (2004). Cultural identity, explanatory style, and depression in Navajo adolescents. *Cultural Diversity and Ethnic Minority Psychology, 10*(4), 365–382.

Robin, R. W., Chester, B., & Rasmussen, J. K. (1998). Intimate violence in a Southwestern American Indian tribal community. *Cultural Diversity and Ethnic Minority Psychology, 4*(4), 335–344.

Taylor, M. J. (2000). The influence of self-efficacy on alcohol use among American Indians. *Cultural Diversity and Ethnic Minority Psychology, 6*(2), 152–167.

Yellow Bird, M. (2004). The continuing effects of American Colonialism upon First Nations Peoples. In A. Lieberman & C. Lester (Eds.), *Social work practice with a difference: Stories, essays, cases, and commentaries* (pp. 272–278). New York: McGraw Hill.

Yellow Horse Brave Heart, M. (2001). Culturally and historically congruent clinical social work assessment with Native clients. In R. Fong & S. Furuto (Eds.), *Culturally competent practice, skills, interventions, and evaluations* (pp. 163–175). Boston: Allyn & Bacon.

3 Spinning Out of Control: The Story of the McFaddens

*Accept all your child's feelings as natural and don't dwell
on whether they make sense.*
Ford, 1995, p. 44

Getting Started

"I feel like I'm living a nightmare. I don't know who my children are anymore. My son is in trouble every other day. He's on the Internet to all hours of the night, and when he goes out I don't know where he's going. I hear him conversing with women, but I never see him bring anyone home. My daughter Katherine used to be such an obedient girl, so quiet and loving; now she tells me she's dating a girl. What's going on with my family? Everyone is out of control!"

What reaction are you aware of right now?

_____

_____

The McFaddens found out about the Interfaith Counseling Center from their neighbor. They have two children, Brian, age seventeen, and Katherine, age sixteen. Margaret, Mrs. McFadden, is married to Timothy, who owns a grocery store in town.

- What is going on here?

  _____

  _____

- What might be your first clinical step during this initial interview?

  _____

  _____

THOUGHTS TO PONDER

Pathological gambling, *DSM-IV* 312.31; Persistent and recurrent maladaptive gambling behavior as indicated by at least five of the following:

The questions exploring maladaptive Internet use in the present study

1. Is preoccupied with gambling (e.g., preoccupied with reliving past gambling experiences, handicapping or planning the next venture, or thinking of ways to get money with which to gamble)

1. I often realize I am only waiting to log on to the Internet again.

2. Needs to gamble with increasing amounts of money in order to achieve the desired excitement

2. I have to use the Internet more and more to experience the excitement.

3. Has repeated unsuccessful efforts to control, cut back, or stop gambling

3. I often try cutting down on the amount of time I spend on the Internet, and fail. OR When I am on the Internet I often decide "just a few more minutes."

4. Is restless or irritable when attempting to cut down or stop gambling

4. I snap, shout, or get irritated if I am bothered with other things when I am using the Internet.

5. Gambles as a way of escaping from problems or of relieving a dysphoric mood (e.g., feelings of helplessness, guilt, anxiety, depression)

5. I want to block out disturbing thoughts about my life with soothing thoughts of the Internet.

6. After losing money in gambling, often returns another day in order to get even ("chasing" one's losses)

6. (not relevant)

7. Lies to family members, therapist, or others to conceal the extent of involvement with gambling

7. I try to hide how much time I spend on the Internet.

8. Has committed illegal acts, such as forgery, fraud, theft, or embezzlement, in order to finance gambling

8. (not relevant)

9. Has jeopardized or lost a significant relationship, job, or education or career opportunity because of gambling

9. I quit homework or domestic duties to be able to spend more time on the Internet. OR I sleep less due to late-night log-ins.

| 10. Relies on others to provide money to relieve a desperate financial situation caused by gambling | 10. (not relevant) |

DSM-IV refers to the Diagnostic and Statistical Manual of Mental Disorders which provides a guide to clinical practice offering classification of mental disorders based on research and field trials.

(Kaltiala-Heino; Lintonen, & Rimpela, 2004, p. 92)

THOUGHTS TO PONDER

"Family therapists need to keep in mind that friendship, community, and workplace sources of social support are as important as family of origin support for a lesbian/gay person's mental health. Many aspects of the therapy—taking a history, constituting a program, formulating the problem, setting goals, deciding whom to include in sessions and referral to adjunct therapeutic and support services—should reflect this expanded social network focus." (Green, 2000, p. 262)

A Window to the Past

Margaret

Margaret, an attractive "black Irish" woman with black hair, blue eyes, and fair skin, was born in Dublin and raised with six sisters and one brother. Her parents lived in a small town where three generations of O'Rileys lived. Margaret attended the local Catholic school and participated in church services weekly. Soon after receiving her first holy communion, she became an altar girl. Later she joined the church choir. She had a natural talent for singing and was often praised for her beautiful voice. Her family was proud of her. She was a quiet girl who obeyed the family rules and followed the Irish traditions. Margaret often felt restricted in her small town and dreamed about moving to the United States and experiencing a big city. She was artistic and musically talented and wanted to pursue a career in the arts. Her parents thought that it was nice as a hobby to pursue her artistic talents, but they guided her toward a more suitable career for a woman that would be helpful following marriage and raising children, such as teaching or nursing. In her last year of high school Margaret began dating Timothy.

Timothy

Timothy, an athletically tall and broad blonde man, was born and raised in Dublin with his parents and four brothers. He is the third youngest of his siblings. He remembers the financial struggles the family endured and recalls the shame of wearing worn-out "hand me downs" from his older brothers. Timothy's father worked in a wool factory as a foreman and his mother was a homemaker. Timothy harbors the memory of heated arguments with his parents when his father drank, yet the family never missed a Sunday mass at the local Catholic Church. Timothy resented his impoverished life, his father's frequent beatings, and his father's criticism of him and his brothers. On several occasions Timothy stole clothing and sometimes bakery goods, but he was never caught. He dreamed of a better life and was determined to leave when he became an adult to join his oldest brother and sister-in-law in the United States. His sister-in-law had a large extended family who had emigrated to the United States ten years earlier.

Margaret and Timothy

Margaret described Timothy as charismatic and charming. He had vivid dreams of going to the United States and living with his brother and sister-in-law "to make it big." Timothy was captured by Margaret's enchanting looks and flair for creativity. They talked about marriage, and Margaret felt this was an opportunity to follow her dream, too. Margaret's father was upset about this marriage and felt that Timothy was a big talker, lazy and not a suitable partner for his daughter. In fact, he had heard that Timothy was gambling and had borrowed money from a friend with no intention of returning it. Margaret did not want to hear such stories about Timothy; she loved him and they were going to the United States to have a blissful life.

Within a year after graduating from high school, Timothy and Margaret married and left Ireland for the United States. Timothy worked as a salesman in his brother's clothing store. They enjoyed living in a big city and spent time going to the theater, dining in new ethnic restaurants, and socializing with friends and family. Katherine was born one year after Timothy and Margaret arrived in the United States, and Brian was born eleven months later. Timothy and Margaret called their children "Irish twins." Birth control was frowned upon by the Catholic Church; therefore many couples often had children close in age. After two years Margaret noticed that Timothy began drinking more than he had when they lived in Ireland. She did not pay much attention to his drinking, however, because her father drank and visiting the pub in the evenings seemed to be an accepted activity.

Margaret also worked in one of her brother-in-law's clothing stores and helped the store start its own line of casual wear by designing various articles of clothing. She was happy designing clothes and continued working part time in the store and part time at home after Brian and Katherine were born.

Timothy was not satisfied with his sales position and felt jealous of Margaret's success with her designs. He spent less time at home and more time at the pub. He began stealing from his brother and was fired. He began attending Alcoholics Anonymous and became active in the program. After a year, he opened a small grocery store with money Margaret had saved. He no longer drinks, he attends church regularly with Margaret and the children, and he has made amends with his brother and family.

THOUGHTS TO PONDER

People who suffer from alcoholism and other addictions usually harbor deep feelings of neglect and abandonment. The addiction soothes the pain temporarily, thus keeping the cycle of abuse active. Learning how to nurture oneself in healthy ways is critical for long-term recovery.

Brian

Brian was an active boy who wanted his own way. He was known to have temper tantrums at a young age, and the tantrums continued into adolescence. Margaret was unable to control him. He would not listen to advice from his uncle or Timothy. Brian began experimenting with marijuana and has become a regular user. Recently he has become obsessed with the Internet and spends hours viewing pornography. He does not feel that he has a problem and states that he is enjoying himself and not harming anyone.

Katherine

Katherine is a responsible student and close to Margaret. She is quiet and protective of Margaret. She worries about her brother, but she does not express anger toward him. She sometimes smokes marijuana with him. She is also close to Timothy and enjoys the love and kindness he brings to the family since his recovery from alcoholism. When she turned thirteen, her friends began expressing interest in boys. She became aware that she did not have amorous feelings toward boys but rather was interested in girls. Katherine fantasized about her best friend Patricia. They kissed a few times, but Katherine does not know where the relationship is going. She was uncomfortable about these feelings and was not able to tell anyone. Being raised as a Catholic girl, she felt it was unclean to have such feelings and she became reclusive. She often would sneak marijuana from Brian's room and smoke in her room with Patricia. She stopped going out with her school and church friends and spent a lot of time reading fashion magazines. She helped in her uncle's store and spent more time with her mother.

- How has the McFaddens' history impacted their lives?

  _____

  _____

- Describe your clinical impressions about the McFadden family members.

  _____

  _____

THOUGHTS TO PONDER

"The short-term or long-term consequences of coming out to parents remain largely unknown at this time. It seems most likely that there are a variety of positive, negative, and mixed family relationship outcomes and that these outcomes are partially a function of the pre-disclosure relationships among family members and the attitudes toward homosexuality prevalent in each family member's sociocultural niche." (Green, 2000, p. 262).

What would be your next step in treatment with Brian and with Katherine?

_____

_____

Exploratory Research and Resource Corner

- What literature and/or resources would be helpful to you at this point?

  _____

  _____

- What homework assignments would you explore to enhance communication?

Embracing the Essence

Family session with Margaret, Timothy, Brian, Katherine, and therapist at the Interfaith Counseling Center. Margaret sits next to Timothy and Katherine sits next to Margaret. Brian sits away from family.

THERAPIST: Welcome to our center. I'm looking forward to working with you and hearing about your challenges.

MARGARET: I hope you can help us; my children have become strangers to me.

THERAPIST: Can you describe what that means, Margaret?

MARGARET: Brian was such a playful and pleasant boy when he was young. Now he smokes marijuana, yells at everyone, and goes out with people we don't know. He spends hours watching pornography on the Internet, and I'm wondering if he's meeting women when he goes out. There are diseases out there, you know. Maybe he's having sex. My God, what could happen these days!

THERAPIST: I'm hearing that you are concerned about Brian and feel confused about what's going on.

BRIAN: She's exaggerating. Yeah, I'm getting high, a little marijuana here and there. No big deal. I'm a growing young man, what's wrong with a little porn, everyone does it.

TIMOTHY: Marijuana is the least of it. I'm worried about sexually transmitted infections, especially AIDS.

BRIAN: (Angrily looks at Timothy, raises his voice.) Why are you picking on me? Why don't you go after Katherine? You think she's such a good Catholic girl. Do you know she's smoking marijuana and kissing girls?

KATHERINE: (Recoils in her chair; feels embarrassed about this open revelation.)

BRIAN: (Continues to raise voice, starts moving restlessly in his chair.) I know you hate me, you think I'm just like dad, I'm a nobody! And you, Katherine, you just sit there all the time hiding out.

THERAPIST: (Feels overwhelmed at this point and feels numb and speechless.)

TIMOTHY: We want to help you, Brian. You don't see what's happening to you.

BRIAN: (Still restless in his chair.) No one knows what I'm feeling; I don't know what to do. (Brian gets up and kicks the wall.)

THERAPIST: (Slowly gets up and walks gently toward him.)

BRIAN: Don't come near me!

MARGARET: This is what we deal with at home; we can't take it anymore.

- As the family therapist, how might you have dealt with this session?

  _____

  _____

- What clinical tools might you use to work with Brian's anger?

  _____

  _____

- What more do you need to know?

  _____

  _____

MINDFUL SELF-REFLECTION MOMENT
Close your eyes; take a breath.

What feelings or thoughts are you aware of?

_____

_____

_____

THERAPIST'S TOOLS

It is important that as therapists we develop the ability to understand and empathize with the client's experience. Unfortunately, our primary tool of "cognition" is limiting and could even be an interference. Often, therapists want to "fix" the problem. This fixing process moves the therapist into "cognitive action," usually in the form of developing tasks to solve the problem. Working with the McFaddens may stimulate various beliefs, opinions, and feelings for the therapist; therefore, multidimensional awareness will open the door for empathy, clarity, and a "loving presence." Another way to move the McFaddens toward healing is to reframe how we "listen." Listening to the storyteller's nonverbal response, gestures, and senses, rather than solely focusing on the story, will intensify the connection with the client/family. How can we facilitate this deeper connection?

1. *Silence.* Therapists can fine-tune their listening tools by letting the client speak until finished, thus allowing time for integration, a connection between feelings and thoughts. Feeling comfortable with moments of silence during this integration and listening to your internal cues will foster a deeper sense of knowing for client and therapist.
2. *Expectations.* When therapists let go of their expectation of how the clinical process and outcome should emerge, only then can they truly be present for the client's experience.
3. *Interpretation.* Too often therapists depend upon theoretical frameworks to "make sense" of what is occurring with the client/family. In so doing, therapists move away from "sensing" what is transpiring, and this moving away often cuts off a central component: "being present" with the client.

TAKE A ONE-MINUTE VACATION

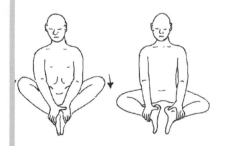

The Open Heart Bring soles of feet together, heels toward groin, and hold the feet. Press sacrum down, lifting top of head away from shoulders. Let knees bounce like the flutter of your heart.

Riding the Wave

Margaret and Timothy felt helpless in dealing with Brian. They could not monitor him all the time, and he felt no remorse for his behavior. Recently they noticed that their phone bill contained multiple calls to 900 numbers for telephone sex and for business cards of clubs that solicit sexual activity. They feel things are spiraling out of control. Margaret and Timothy were shocked about Katherine's sexual orientation and felt ashamed to discuss it with the family. They sought out help from their parish priest, who recommended that they pray for Katherine and bring her to a Bible study group to deepen her faith. Katherine became more of a recluse and went to Bible studies unwillingly and with feelings of shame because she felt she was being punished for her sexual orientation. She began to develop obsessive thoughts about being unclean and spent a lot of time taking long baths and washing her clothes. Her behavior went unnoticed by Margaret, who thought she would get over her "lesbian problem" and come to her senses.

- Describe your concerns about Katherine. What would be your next step?

  _____

  _____

- What do you know about obsessive-compulsive disorder? What are the developmental milestones to consider in working with Katherine?

  _____

  _____

THOUGHTS TO PONDER

Suggestions to help Brian regain control of his Internet use:

Request a time log. Ask for a written log of the hours children spend online each day, including a list of what was done (e.g., chatting, e-mailing, using instant messages). Do not allow your child to eliminate the computer's history log.

Establish clear limits. Set rules about the number of hours that your children can be online. If they disobey the rules, you may have to change the log-on password to control their Internet access.

Keep the computer in a common area. Place the computer in your dining or living room and walk by several times while your children are online to let them know they are being monitored. Keep the modem with you if your teen gets home before you do. You may also want to keep the modem in your bedroom at night. If your child has a wireless computer, you might keep it in a place that is locked.

Encourage real-time activities. Help your children reconnect with groups they previously enjoyed or encourage them to explore new interests.

Talk to your child's teachers. Share your concerns with your child's teachers and guidance counselors. They can help by watching for any changes in behavior, monitoring Internet use at school, and keeping you informed of any assignments that require use of the Internet. (Shriner, 2002, p. 3)

Celebrating Family Culture

The McFadden family felt strongly about its family tradition of keeping private affairs at home. To understand the historical lineage of the McFaddens, one must look at the values of a typical Irish Catholic family. Raising a large family is important. Wilson Davis's (1980) study of 719 Roman Catholic Irish wives under forty-four years old found that the family preference size was 4.3 children. With acculturation to the United States, the Irish family changed from poor, uneducated farmers to educated and economically successful people. Adhering to the advice of the local parish priest and traditions of the church has been an integral part of life for Irish Catholic families. Also, the strong role of the Irish mother sets the tone for family expectations and values.

Raising a lesbian adolescent poses a variety of stresses upon the McFadden family given their faith and cultural beliefs. Garofalo, Wolf, Kellel, Palfrey, and DuRant (1998) studied over 4000 gay, lesbian, and bisexual ninth-through twelfth-grade public high school adolescents. They found that youth who self-identify were at a greater health risk for problem behaviors such as suicide and victimization, sexual risk behaviors, and multiple substance use (p. 895). Garofalo, Wolf, Wissow, Woods and Goodman (1999) studied 129 gay, lesbian, and bisexual youth and others who were ambivalent about their sexual preference and found that the individuals studied reported a significant increase in suicide attempts. Armestos (2001) studied 356 gay and lesbian youth and asked them to imagine that they were the parents of an adolescent who recently disclosed his or her alternative sexual orientation. He found that there was a higher tendency to experience shame than guilt.

Margaret and Timothy decided to follow their priest's advice with Katherine and believed that with prayers and spiritual guidance she would become heterosexual. They felt that Katherine's solitude was a good sign and did not see Katherine's emerging obsessive behaviors. They interpreted her solitude as a sign of repentance.

Green (2000) suggests that therapists not encourage gay, lesbian, and bisexual clients to come out to their families if they choose not to. He states that their decision should be viewed as a healthy one and not a result of poor mental health or lack of differentiation from the family. Social support for a lesbian/gay person and for the couple relationship is important for mental health whether or not the person comes out to the family (p. 263).

Brian admitted that he felt judged by the parochial school priests and by Margaret and Timothy for interfering in his decision to pursue viewing pornography. He decided not to attend parochial school when he was suspended for using the school's computers for porn, and he questioned his faith entirely. Dealing with Brian's excessive use of the Internet and exposure to pornography poses a major challenge for the McFaddens. Research in the United States found that teens use the Internet more than adults (Subrahmanyam, Kraut, Greenfied, & Gross, 2001). Wolak, Mitchell, and Finkelhor (2002) found that boys who had poor communication with their parents or were highly troubled were more likely to form close relationships online. They also found that among American youth ten to seventeen years old who were regular Internet users, 25 percent had been exposed to unwanted sexual pictures. Finkelhor, Mitchell, and Wolak's (2000) survey of American youth found that 19 percent of Internet users ten to seventeen years old received unwanted sexual solicitation. Greenfield (1998) studied 18,000 Internet users who logged onto the American Broadcasting System (ABC) News Web site. He found that 62 percent said they regularly logged onto pornography sites, that individuals spent an average of four hours a week online, and that 37.5 percent reported masturbating while online. Cooper notes that men prefer visual stimuli and more focused sexual experiences, which may account for the higher percentage of men visiting pornography sites than women (who were more likely to spend time flirting or having cybersex in chat rooms). (De Angelis, 2000)

The McFaddens are struggling with the traditional values and beliefs of their Irish Catholic heritage while trying to understand the lifestyle choices of their children.

- What might Margaret and Timothy be feeling?

- How would you deal with Brian's pornography obsession?

- What are your thoughts about the priest's advice for Katherine?

• How have the McFaddens' culture and religious beliefs impacted their perceptions and lifestyle?

_____

_____

MINDFUL SELF-REFLECTION MOMENT
Close your eyes; take a breath.

What feelings or thoughts are you aware of?

_____

_____

_____

TAKE A ONE-MINUTE VACATION

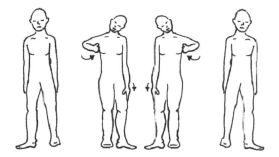

Monkey Stand with feet slightly wider than shoulder width apart, bend knees a bit, and relax arms at side. Press soles of feet into the ground, squeeze the buttocks, and exhale "ha!" making fist with left hand and sliding it into the left armpit while your right hand slides down the right leg. Allow torso to bend to the right and lean into the right leg for support. Inhale, return to center, and repeat on other side several times, going side to side.

Beyond Treatment

The McFaddens feel that they have sought out help from the treatment center and their parish priest. Aside from the family program at the Interfaith
Counseling Center, they feel that they have done their job and the children
will move on with their lives. From a prevention perspective,

- What else needs to happen?

  _____

  _____

- Would you recommend that any member of the McFaddens be seen by
  the therapist individually? If so, why or why not?

  _____

  _____

- Discuss what resources you might explore with the McFadden family at
  this point.

  _____

  _____

REFERENCES

Armestos, J. C. (2001). Attributions and emotional reactions to the identity disclosure ("Com-
ing out") of a homosexual child. *Family Process, 40*(2), 145–161.
Finkelhor, D., Mitchell, K. J., & Wolak, J. (2000). Online victimization: A report on the nation's
youth, viewed October 31, 2003, http://www.unh.edu/ccrc/pdf/Victimization_Online_
Survey.pdf.
Ford, J. (1995). *Wonderful ways to love a child,* Emerville, CA: Conari Press, p. 44.
Garofalo, R., Wolf, R. C., Kessel, S., Palfrey, J., & DuRant, R. H. (1998). The association between health risk behaviors and sexual orientation among a school-based sample of
adolescents. *Pediatrics, 101*(5), 895–902.
Garofalo, R., Wolf, R. C., Wissow, L. S., Woods, E. R., & Goodman, E. (1999). Sexual orientation and risk of suicide attempts among a representative sample of youth. *Archives Pediatric Adolescent Medicine, 153*(5), 487–493.
Green, R. J. (2000). Lesbians, gay men and their parents: A critique of LaSala and the pre-
vailing clinical wisdom. *Family Process, 39*(2), 257–266.
Greenfield, D. (1998). Center for Internet Studies (www.virual-addiction.com).
Subrahmanyam, K., Kraut, R., Greenfield, P., & Gross, E. (2001). New forms of electronic
media. In D. G. Singer & J. L. Singer (Eds.), *Handbook of children and the media* (pp.
73–99). Thousand Oaks, CA: Sage.
Wolak, J., Mitchell, K. J., & Finkelhor, D. (2002). Close online relationships in a national
sample of adolescents. *Adolescence, 37*(147), 441–455.

SUGGESTED READING

Bennett, M. J. (2001). *The empathic healer, an endangered species?* San Diego, California: Academic Press.

Bontempo, D. E., & D'Augellli, A. R. (2002). Effects of at-school victimization and sexual orientation of lesbian, gay, or bisexual youth's health risk behavior. *Journal of Adolescent Health, 30*(5), 364–374.

De Angelis, T. (2000). Is Internet addiction real? *Monitor on Psychology, 31*(4).

Fischer, R. L. (2004). Assessing client change in individual and family counseling. *Social Work Practice, 14*(2), 102–111.

Fleming, M., & Rickwood, D. (2004). Teens in cyberspace: Do they encounter friend or foe? *Youth Studies Australia, 23*(3), 46–51.

Inglis, T. (2001). Honour, pride and shame in rural Ireland. *Amsterdam Sociologisch Tijdschrift, 28*(4), 495–512.

Kaltiala-Heino, R., Lintonen, T., & Rimpela, J. (2004). Internet addiction? Potential use of the internet in a population of 12–18 year old adolescents. *Addiction Research and Theory, 12*(1), 89–96.

Lantz, J. (2004). World view concepts in existential family therapy. *Contemporary Family Therapy, 26*(2), 165–178.

LaRose, R., Mastro, D., & Eastin, M. S. (2001). Understanding Internet usage: A social-cognitive approach to uses and gratifications. *Social Science Computer Review, 19*(4), 395–413.

LaSala, M. C. (2000). Lesbians, gay men and their parents: Family therapy for the coming-out crisis. *Family Process, 39*(1), 67–81.

Miller, R. (2002). *The matriarchal maintenance of family continuity under conditions of high political and domestic stress.* Paper presented at the Conference of the International Sociological Association, Brisbane, Australia. Accession Number 2004SO1364.

Mitchell, K. J., Finkelhor, D., & Wolak, J. (2003). The exposure of youth to unwanted sexual material on the Internet. *Youth and Society, 34*(3), 330–358.

Robin, L., Brener, N. D., Donahue, S. F., Hack, T., Hale, K., & Gonenow, C. (2002). Associations between health risk behaviors and opposite-, same-both-sex sexual partners in representative samples of Vermont and Massachusetts high school students. *Archive Pediatric Adolescent Medicine, 156*(4), 349–355.

Rosario, M., Schrimshaw, E. W., & Hunter, J. (2004). Ethnic/racial differences in the coming-out process of lesbian, gay and bisexual youth: A comparison of sexual identity development over time. *Cultural Diversity and Ethnic Minority Psychology, 10*(3), 215–228.

Saulnier, C. F. (2002). Decide who to see: Lesbians discuss their preferences in health and mental health care providers. *Journal of the National Association of Social Workers, 47*(4), 355–365.

Seaward, B. L. (2004). Behavior modification. In *Managing stress: Principles and strategies for health and well-being* (pp. 202–214). Sudbury, MA: Jones and Bartlett Publishers.

Shaffer, H. J., Hall, M. N., & Vander Bilt, J. (2000). Computer addiction: A critical consideration. *American Journal of Orthopsychiatry, 70*(2), 162–168.

Shriner, J. A. (2002). Untangling the web for internet addicted adolescents. Family Life Month Packet, 2002; Family and consumer Sciences, Ohio Sate University Extension, The Ohio State University. (http://www.hec.ohio-state.edu/famlif/)

Whitlock, E., Orleans, T., Pender, N., & Allan, J. (2002). Evaluating primary care behavioral counseling interventions: An evidence-based approach. *American Journal of Preventive Medicine, 22*(4), 267–284.

Wilson-Davis, K. (1980). Ideal family size in the Irish republic. *Journal of Biosocial Science, 12*(1), 15–20.

4 Down with Depression: The Story of the Polanskys

The only rejection that has any power is self-rejection. You have been taught that life must define your experience rather than that your experiences are creating your life. You look outside to seek yourself.

Rodegast & Stanton, 1989, p. 67

Getting Started

"My son Barry is twenty-two years old and sleeps all day, stays up all night, and never leaves the house. He's always been a shy and quiet boy. I don't know when he last took a shower; it must be at least two weeks. My husband is out of his skin. He's an old-fashioned man and wants to throw Barry out of the house to make a man of him. What's happening to our son?"

What reaction are you aware of right now?

_____

_____

Barry is the second oldest of two boys born to Bella and Sidney, Russian Jews who emigrated to the United States when they were adolescents. Their oldest son David recently graduated from an Ivy League college and is beginning his master's degree in engineering. Barry did well in high school but had difficulty adjusting to college. He completed one semester and dropped out the second semester and returned home. He has taken odd jobs for short periods of time. For the past year he has been at home, unemployed, and does not leave the house.

What do you know about depression?

_____

_____

A Window into the Past

Bella

Bella was born and raised in Lithuania, during the communist regime. Her father Aaron was a physician and her mother Anna was an engineer. Before the communist regime, Bella's parents lived a comfortable life. Bella's grandfather owned several businesses, and Bella's parents enjoyed the intimacy of extended family. During the pogroms Bella's maternal grandparents lost all of their family possessions and their businesses were taken over by the Russian government. Bella's grandparents and mother, who was an adolescent at the time, were sent to Siberia to live in "work camps," which were better known to everyone as "concentration camps." Her maternal grandmother died of starvation while living there. Her grandfather survived and developed a deep resentment for the Russian government.

During World War II Anna lost most of her family in the Holocaust. She reported that the family never believed Hitler would invade Russia due to the peace treaty between Germany and Russia at that time. The German invasion occurred overnight. Anna had a large extended family that included several sisters and one brother; miraculously she survived by living in the basement of a friend's apartment for most of the war.

After several decades, they were able to escape to France and a year later came to the United States. Bella's mother Anna was married to Aaron, and Bella was their only child. She was thirteen years old when they arrived in New York.

Bella had a gift for language and easily learned English. She attended high school and had a few close friends. They lived in a Russian immigrant community that provided ample opportunity for Russian traditions to continue. Bella attended a local college, where she received her degree in radiology. She met Sidney in the college cafeteria. They were married a year after she graduated.

If you were Bella growing up, describe what you may have experienced during those earlier years.

_____

_____

Sidney

Sidney was born and raised in Moscow. He is the older of two children. His sister, Natasha, is three years his junior. His father Uri was a foreman in an automobile factory and his mother Toby was a homemaker. Toby suffered from depression, which had gone unnoticed. She spent most of her time at home due to the cold weather. Shopping for the bare necessities was all that was required for lack of money and the unavailability of goods in stores. Sidney's family survived World War II but not unscathed. His parents were sent to a concentration camp after being captured toward the end of the war.

Toby had been a frail and gentle woman who lived a sheltered life. Her experiences from the war scarred her for life. She mourned for her friends and extended family members who died. Toby felt guilty at times for surviving. She became depressed following the war and often ruminated about the horrors she experienced. On the other hand, Uri had a "fight to live" and was determined to escape the oppression he felt living in Russia.

Sidney's family lived in the city of Moscow until Sidney was twelve years old, when they emigrated to the United States. They lived with Uri's cousin Joshua, who was able to obtain a working visa for Uri as a mechanic in a specialty foreign car dealership. Sidney attended the neighborhood schools. Natasha mastered English easily, but English did not come easily for Sidney and he experienced teasing and ridicule during his middle and high school years. He was able to complete his college education in business administration while attending night school and working during the day with his father and uncle changing oil and tires. When Sidney met Bella in the cafeteria, he knew instantly that this was the woman he wanted to spend the rest of his life with. Toby's depression became more noticeable when they moved to the United States. She missed her sisters, who were a constant source of support for her.

What experiences might Sidney have had upon arriving to the United States?

_____

_____

Sidney and Bella

Bella was a shy girl who was instantly captured by Sidney's tall, dark, handsome looks and assertive manner. He was five years older than Bella. She dated him against her parent's advice. They had aspirations that Bella would marry a physician, like her father Aaron. There were many arguments in which her parents complained that Sidney was not a suitable husband for her. Bella married Sidney regardless, hoping that her parents would eventually let go of their resentment. After three years of marriage, Bella gave birth to David and two years later Barry. Bella continued to work as a radiologist and Sidney continued to work for his cousin Joshua. He felt that he owed his cousin since he helped his family and kept them employed following their arrival from Russia. Sidney was promoted to manager of sales and enjoyed his job; he felt that he had earned the position. Sidney was much like his father Uri, determined to make a better life for himself and enjoy the benefits of freedom. He often sent clothing to relatives in Moscow, who were not fortunate enough to leave or escape for a better life.

What factors may have influenced Anna and Aaron's feelings about Sidney?

_____

_____

David

David, twenty-four years old, was Bella and Sidney's pride and joy. He was charming as a child and had a jovial sense of humor. He was inquisitive and bright and learned how to read by the time he was four. He enjoyed playing baseball, was a gifted flautist, and his ability for mathematics earned him a partial scholarship to an Ivy League university. He continued on to law school and has a successful practice with a large law firm. He is close to the family yet maintains a very active social life. He is also quite the Romeo and enjoys many female relationships.

Barry

Barry, twenty-two years old, is two years younger than David. He was a quiet child and was attached to Bella. He didn't like loud noises, had fears early in his development (for example, he couldn't sleep without a night light), was afraid of thunder, and was intimidated by his father's loud voice. Bella felt a need to protect Barry. Barry spent a lot of time alone and enjoyed building. When he was a boy he spent hours using blocks and kits to build airplanes, trains, buildings, ships, and anything that fancied his imagination. He enjoyed helping Sidney repair electrical appliances and was fascinated about how things 'worked.' Barry often asked questions about the car engines in his cousin's dealership. Both Bella and Sidney observed Barry's talents and had dreams of Barry becoming an engineer, like Anna, Bella's mother.

Barry had a small group of friends throughout elementary and high school who were known as the "school nerds." They enjoyed science and spent most of their time exploring and developing various projects. They often worked on group projects and won many awards throughout their school years. Barry had an exceptional ability to improve and sophisticate the projects using his imagination and ability for small detail. He did not date in high school and attended a local college. He dropped out of college after his first semester. He took a job in an electronics store. He enjoyed being around the merchandise yet felt socially anxious around the customers. He remained close to Bella and his small group of friends, some of whom left the community to attend college.

Barry's shyness began to appear more like withdrawal from social events, and recently he became completely isolated and was reluctant to leave the house. He has not worked in eighteen months. Bella and Sidney encourage him to finish school, but Barry seems to have difficulty interacting with people outside of his family. He sleeps during the day and is up at night. He has lost weight and mopes around. He likes to read and has visited the library several times a week to check out books. Recently he has not left the house and refuses to leave, stating that he has no energy and wants to stay at home. He feels there's nothing "out there for him." He does not show any interest in the activities he had and in fact has several incomplete projects sitting in the family garage.

- How would you deal with Barry's depression?

  _____

  _____

- What are some challenges children of survivors face?

  _____

  _____

- Describe what might be your next step in working with the Polanskys.

  _____

  _____

THOUGHTS TO PONDER

"Strictly speaking, the shadow is the repressed part of the ego and represents what we are unable to acknowledge about ourselves. The body that hides beneath clothes often blatantly expresses what we consciously deny. In the image we present to others, we often do not want to show our anger, our anxiety, our sadness, our constrictedness, our depression, or our need." (Conger, 1991, p. 85)

Exploratory Research and Resource Corner

- What would help you understand Bella and Sidney's family experience in Russia?

  _____

  _____

- Where might you find professionals who can offer you information to help you work with the Polanksys?

  _____

  _____

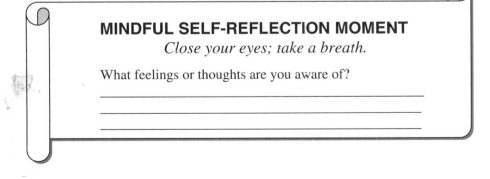

MINDFUL SELF-REFLECTION MOMENT
Close your eyes; take a breath.

What feelings or thoughts are you aware of?

_____

_____

_____

Embracing the Essence

First Family Session (Bella, Sidney, Barry, Therapist)

Bella and Sidney Polansky brought Barry to his first session at the Jewish Community Mental Health Center. Barry had not been away from the house for two months. With much encouragement he had showered, brushed his teeth, and put on clean clothes, which Bella washed the night before the appointment.

During this session Barry sat with his head down and did not speak a word. Bella did most of the talking, sharing stories of his projects and friends. Sidney was more agitated than supportive. He complained about Barry being lazy and "a momma's boy" and he reported that it was high time for him to grow up and be a man. Barry sank deeper into his chair.

- What is Bella's role in the family?

  _____

  _____

- How would you deal with Sidney's agitation?

  _____

  _____

- What are your clinical impressions regarding Barry's situation?

  _____

  _____

- What would you do if you were the therapist?

  _____

  _____

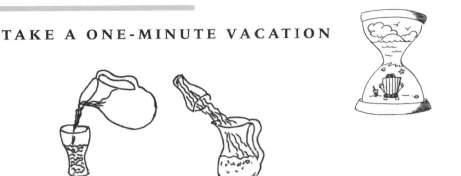

TAKE A ONE-MINUTE VACATION

Three-Part Breath The three-part breath focuses on the three parts of your lungs: the tummy (the bottom part), the ribs and middle chest, and the upper chest and shoulders. It helps clear air out of the top of your lungs, where stale air often is stored that needs to be let out. When you breathe into these chambers of your body, you will experience the most complete breath. To fully understand how air comes in and out of your lungs, think about how water fills up a glass. It first goes into the bottom and fills up to the top; when emptied it first empties from the top and then the bottom. Imagine that your lungs are like the glass.

Celebrating Family Culture

The Polanskys have lived through many hardships. Life in Russia left many scars for both Sidney and Bella. Historically, the rights of Jews and the hostility toward them in Russia date back to the fifteenth century and continue today. Before the communist regime, Bella's grandparents and great grandparents were among the "Russian Jewish 'intelligentsia' which acquired the Russian language, Russian culture and strove to integrate and assimilate into Russian Society" (Ettinger, 1971, p. 101). Ettinger notes that after the Revolution of 1917 the political activism of Jews disintegrated. The events of World War I and the Holocaust of World War II added to the oppression of Russian Jews. In order to assimilate into the Russian society, Jews had to suppress their identity or protest against national suppression. During the 1960s Russian Jews strove to become involved in developing the state of Israel, particularly the younger generation of the 1960s, on whom the Six Day War made a lasting impression.

Leaving Russia for Israel enhanced the Russian Jew's chance for survival and for preservation of Jewish identity. In Israel Russian Jews could practice Judaism and identify with their culture without oppression and secrecy. The United States also provided Russian Jews the hope of a homeland of freedom, yet discrimination and oppression prevailed and many Jews changed their names, synagogues were desecrated, and the identity of being Jewish was kept secret.

To understand the coping patterns in families of Holocaust survivors, Chaitlin (2003) describes several types of families—victim families, fighter families, numb families, and "those who made it"—as a result of an exploratory study interviewing fifty-seven individuals from twenty families who represented two to three generations of survivors of the Holocaust. For the Polanskys we see identification with two of these profiles.

Victim families' survivors are characterized by pervasive depression, worry, and mistrust and fear of the outside world, accompanied by symbiotic clinging within the family. These families are concerned mostly with survival and often live in fear of another Holocaust. Survivor parents regard the setting of boundaries and expression of independence by their children as a threat to the family unit. It seems that Sidney's mother Toby and, subsequently, Barry have characteristics of this type of family dynamic.

Fighter families' survivors are characterized by an intense drive for achievement. Family members must always be in control and there is no room for depression or weakness. The most fiercely held virtue is pride; relaxation is perceived of as a waste of time. Children are encouraged to withstand stress and to overcome obstacles (Chaitlin, 2003, p. 1546). Sidney, like his father, fit this profile. Sidney's intolerance of Barry's depression, which Sidney viewed as weakness, may be rooted in his survival mechanism.

The historical theme of depression beginning with Barry's paternal grandmother Toby and continuing with Barry deserves some attention as a family theme. Wingert, Kantrowitz, Braiker, Springen, and Pierce (2002) note that most of the nearly 3 million adolescents struggling with depression never get the help they need because of prejudice about mental illness. Barry most likely was suffering with depression long before it was identified. Sidney's philosophy of "be a man" may have further moved Barry into a depression. Lawson (2004) notes that parents often think that giving boys too much attention and love will result in dependent and clingy kids, especially in their relationships with their mothers. Miller (2002) notes that 20 out of 100 people born experience some form of depression. Marano (2003) notes that three-quarters of depressed adolescents experience further psychiatric disorder. By age twenty-four, half of them have had another episode of depression and another 25 percent have experienced alcohol and drug problems.

Wingert and colleagues (2002) note that without treatment, depressed adolescents are at high risk for school failure, social isolation, promiscuity, "self-medication" with drugs or alcohol, and suicide—now the third leading cause of death among individuals between the ages of ten and twenty-four. "Both antidepressant medication and cognitive-behavior therapy (talk therapy that helps patients identify and deal with sources of stress) have enabled many teenagers to focus on school and resume their lives." (p. 53)

The Polanskys' struggle as survivors and Barry's depression pose many challenges for the family and therapist.

- How has the Polanskys' historical experience of oppression impacted them today?

  _____

  _____

- Describe the strengths some Holocaust survivors develop as a result of their experience.

  _____

  _____

THERAPIST'S TOOLS

As family therapists, we enter the profession with a desire to help families develop or resume harmony. Many people live from "the outside in," that is, largely depending upon outside influences to direct their attitudes and behavior. To truly understand ourselves we need to begin our journey of life "living from the inside out." In doing so, we first check in with ourselves and experience how we feel, what our instincts tell us, how our bodies are responding, and what our senses tell us. When outside stimuli approach, we are prepared with an armory of tools to help us decide what feels good and bad. In working with the Polanskys, it can be a challenge to witness Barry's stagnation. A therapist's "rescue pilot" may come rushing in. In addition, countertransference, the therapist's feeling and reactions that arise toward clients can easily take the therapist on a rollercoaster ride when working with the Polasnskys.

With the plethora of incoming information combined with the stimulation of emotions, it is no wonder that family therapists are continually dealing with "emotional sparks" that erupt and often create interference in the therapeutic relationship. Too often, the therapist's countertransference not only interferes in the family/therapist treatment process but also sets up the therapist for burnout. How can family therapists capture the essence of "being present" with clients and "get out of their own way"?

1. _Embracing your essence._ Letting go of our ego and embracing experiences that are not related to our identity as a therapist, such as laughing with our clients or deeply feeling the warmth of a client's love for his or her child, allows us as therapists to feel more complete and frees our energy that might otherwise be used to fight off feelings or thoughts. When therapists pay attention to their experiences in the moment, the client intuitively senses that the therapist is with him or her in essence, in heart.

2. *Resistance.* Too often therapists get caught up in challenging the family's resistance to change. The conflictual duality a client experiences of outer self, "I want to make this change," and inner self, "I need to hold onto old beliefs preventing me from making this change," is a challenge for families. As therapists, we must maintain a neutral stance, remain present in the process, and allow clients to move through their challenges.

- Describe the generational patterns that you are aware of with the Polanskys.

  _____

  _____

- Explore how these patterns impact their lives today.

  _____

  _____

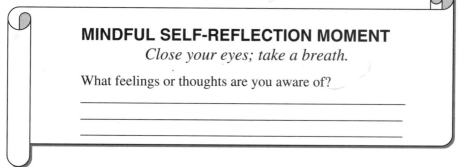

MINDFUL SELF-REFLECTION MOMENT
Close your eyes; take a breath.

What feelings or thoughts are you aware of?

_____

_____

_____

Riding the Wave

First session with Barry and therapist

The therapist asked to see Barry alone the following week. Barry agreed, and Bella brought him to the session. She hesitantly sat in the waiting room. During the session Barry was withdrawn and appeared anxious. He seemed to stare into space when asked a question about how he was feeling. The therapist decided to ask simple, open-ended questions about what he did while at home. Barry reported that he spent a lot of time in his room. He stayed up all night when everyone else was sleeping, ate with the family for dinner, and slept most of the day. He reported watching television, eating potato chips, and drinking soda, and when he felt more energized he read. He liked it when everything was quiet. There were long silences during the first session, and not much more was discussed. The therapist held that space for Barry, hoping to develop some trust.

Describe how you deal with silence during a session?

_____

_____

Second session with Barry, Bella, and Sidney (Barry sits close to his mother; Sidney sits next to Bella on the other side)

THERAPIST: (Shakes Sidney and Bella's hand.) I'm looking forward to working together.

SIDNEY: I hope you can do something with him; we don't seem to know what to do.

THERAPIST: It must be difficult to see your son suffer.

SIDNEY: He doesn't know what real suffering is. We have the life of luxury living here in the United States. I don't know why he can't function.

BELLA: Barry tries; it's just difficult for him.

BARRY: (Sinks deeper into his chair.)

THERAPIST: It's impossible to measure someone's pain.

SIDNEY: I just wish he could get well.

THERAPIST: Barry has many strengths and talents that are camouflaged by his depression. (Turns to Sidney.) Can you take a moment and reflect upon your experience with Barry before he became depressed? Take a few slow breaths; take your time.

SIDNEY: (Sits quietly, anxious at first, and then relaxes; he begins to smile.) I remember how much fun Barry and I had building with his Legos. One project stands out in my mind; we built an airport that took up half of his room; I miss those days.

BARRY: (Looks up at dad, eyes are watery)

THERAPIST: Sidney, can you switch places with Bella?

SIDNEY: (sits next to Barry)

THERAPIST: Can you tell Barry what feelings you are aware of right now?

SIDNEY: (looks at Barry) I miss those days, son. Sometimes I feel that you are just disappearing. I feel so powerless and that scares me.

BARRY: I miss me too.

SIDNEY: Maybe we can go to the library together this week.

BARRY: I would like that.

BELLA: This is a grand day for us, thank you.

Second Session with Barry and Therapist

During this session Barry was a bit more talkative. He shared that during the week his parents were working and he was asked to let the plumbers in to fix a leak in the bathroom. He reported that it took the entire morning for him to think about how he would approach them and what to say. He had not spoken to a stranger in over a year. He thinks people will say negative things to him and talk behind his back. He even practiced going back and forth to the door and bathroom before they came. The therapist asked what was uncomfortable about this encounter. Barry reported that he felt the workers would laugh at him and say negative things about him.

THERAPIST: It's good to see you again, Barry. How are things going?

BARRY: I don't know; I had to let the plumbers in the house to fix the bathroom.

THERAPIST: Were you concerned about this?

BARRY: You know how these guys are, I thought they'd laugh at me, say, what's a nerd Jew boy doing home in the middle of the day?

THERAPIST: Can you describe what made you think the plumbers would mock you?

BARRY: I'm different than everyone else.

THERAPIST: I hear your fear. Barry, can you take a minute? Close your eyes, take a breath, and let yourself listen to what's going on inside. Take your time. (Waits for about two minutes.)

BARRY: (Face softens, body slumps forward.) You know my father talks about how people were shot in the camps if they didn't work. They were useless, a lot like me.

THERAPIST: I'm hearing that you feel useless because you are not working now.

BARRY: That's right, I see how my father looks at me, like I'm dirt, maybe he wants to shoot me, like those Nazis. It was tough in Russia, no decent food, money scarce.

THERAPIST: I wonder if your father understands how much you want to work yet how difficult it is for you to be around people.

BARRY: No, he's a go getter, not like me, you know, my grandmother Toby, his mother, was depressed; dad says I'm just like her.

- Would you consider occasionally seeing Barry at home or outside in a park to help with his anxiety?

_____

_____

- Describe how you might proceed in therapy with Barry.

_____

_____

THOUGHTS TO PONDER

"When you consider what you would love to accomplish in your life but feel ill-prepared to bring it about, picture the eighty-nine-year-old Michelangelo living five centuries ago, painting, sculpting, and writing. Imagine he is telling you that you can create whatever you desire, and the great danger is not in having too much hope, but in reaching what you have perceived as hopeless." (Dyer, 1998, p. 58)

Exploratory Research and Research Corner

- What homework assignments or activities might you explore to empower Barry?

_____

_____

- What resources might you explore?

_____

_____

Beyond Treatment

Barry has been suffering with depression and anxiety, which have emotionally paralyzed him. He is making progress in small increments. Bella and Sidney are working hard to understand Barry and themselves. Barry's brother David has offered to spend time at home with Barry as a support. Although Barry has difficulty getting out, he has taken small steps. For example, after two months of therapy, he went alone to get a haircut and walks at least once a week to the library to check out books; sometimes Sidney goes with him.

He's developed an interest in architectural drafting and has read several books on the subject. He also ventured out to the local grocery store to buy his snacks and is doing his laundry. Bella thought it would be a good idea for family members and Barry's friends to come by individually at different times to visit because this would offer Barry an opportunity to socialize without having to venture out. Barry's birthday is approaching and Bella would like to have a celebration.

- If you were the therapist, what direction would you take to move Barry toward becoming a more autonomous adult?

  _____

  _____

- How would you engage Barry's family in his treatment and recovery?

  _____

  _____

- Would you make a home visit? Describe.

  _____

- What are your thoughts about Bella's idea of a birthday celebration?

  _____

  _____

MINDFUL SELF-REFLECTION MOMENT
Close your eyes; take a breath.

What feelings or thoughts are you aware of?

_____

_____

_____

REFERENCES

Chaitlin, J. (2003). "Living with" the past: Coping and patterns in families of holocaust survivors. *Family Process, 42*(2), 1545–5300.

Conger, J. P (1991). The Body as shadow in Zweig C. & Abrams, J. *Meeting the Shadow: The Hidden Power of the Dark Side of Human Nature.* Penguin Putnam Inc, NY.

Dyer, W. W. (1998). *Wisdom of the Ages: A Modern Master Brings Eternal Truths into Everyday Life,* Harper/Collins. New York.

Ettinger, S. (1971). The roots of soviet and anti-Semitism and the struggle of the Jews. *Dispersion and Unity, 12*(13/14) 101–113.

Miller, M. C. (2003) How genes Affect Moods. *Newsweek.* December 8, p. 70.

Wingert, P., Kantrowitz, B., Braiker, B., Springen, K., & Pierce, E. (2002). Young and depressed. *Newsweek,* October.

SUGGESTED READING

Bride, B. E., Robinson, M. M., Yegidis, B., & Figley, C. R. (2004). Development and validation of the Secondary Traumatic Stress Scale. *Research on Social Work Practice, 14*(1), pp. 27–35.

Green, M. (2003). Interventions with traumatized adolescents. *Annals of Adolescent Psychiatry, 27,* Issue 1, 283–305.

Jones, J. (2003). Saving kids from despair. *School Library Journal,* August. p. 46–49.

Kornblatt, J. D. (1999). Ladies' tailor and the end of Soviet Jewry. *Jewish Social Studies, 5*(3) 180–195.

Lerner, B. (2001). Transcending terror: A study of holocaust survivors' lives. *Dissertation Abstracts International, A: The Humanities and Social Sciences, 61*(9), 3510-A–3511-A.

Levine, S. (2000). The Tao and Talmud of adolescence and young adulthood: Being belonging, believing, benevolence. In *Adolescent Psychiatry, The Annals of the American Society for Adolescent Psychiatry,* (Vol. 25, pp. 45–48). The Analytic Press. Hillsite, N. J.

Nichols, M. P., & Schwartz, R. C. (2004). Bowen Family Systems Therapy. In (Ed.), *Family therapy: Concepts and methods* (pp. 119–148).

O'Connor, T. S. J., Davis, A., Meakes, E., Pickering, R., & Schuman, M. (2004). Narrative therapy using a reflecting team: An ethnographic study of therapists' experiences. *Contemporary Family Therapy, 26*(1), p. 23–39

Petrovsky-Shtern, Y. (2002). *Kritika: Explorations in Russian and Eurasian History 3*(2), 217–254.

Robison, J. I., Wolfe, K., & Edwards, L. (2004). Holistic nutrition: Nourishing the body, mind, and spirit. *Complementary Health Practice Review, 9*(1), 11–20.

Rodegast, P., & Stanton, J. (1989). *Emmanuel's book II: The choice for love.* New York: Bantam Books.

Russinova, Z., Wewiorski, N. J., & Cash, D. (2002). Use of alternative health care practices by persons with serious mental illness: Perceived benefits. *American Journal of Public Health, 92*(10).

Schaub, B. G., & Dossey, B. M. (2000). Imagery: Awakening the inner healer. In (Ed.), *Holistic nursing: A handbook for practice* (pp. 539–579).

Solzhenitsyn, A. (2003). Two hundred years together. *Common Knowledge, 9*(2), 204–227.

Vasquez, A., Manso, G., & Cannell, J. (2004). The clinical importance of vitamin D (cholecalciferol): A paradigm shift with implications for all healthcare providers. *Alternative Therapies in Health and Medicine, 10*(5), 28–36.

Zeuss, J. (1999) The Wisdom of Depression: A Guide to Understanding and Curing Depression Using Natural Medicine. Three Rivers Press.

5 A Gambler Loses It All: The Story of the Williamses

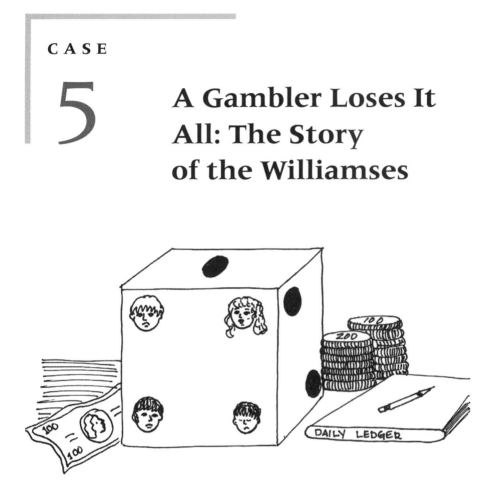

*Confession of error is like a broom that sweeps away dirt
and leaves the surface cleaner than before.*

M. K. Gandhi

Getting Started

"How could I have not known what was happening? I feel as if I'm married to a stranger. He stole from his friends and employers and lied to us. I don't believe I can ever trust him again."

What reactions are you aware of right now?

_____

_____

Ritchie is a forty-five-year-old accountant. He has two sons, Frank and Marcos, ages ten and six. When Ritchie first entered treatment, he was married to his wife Carmen and described having a compulsive gambling problem. He presented as a very clean-cut, all-American kind of guy. Based on his courteous presentation, it was difficult to believe what he was about to say. He stated that he had just returned from being on the road for three weeks. He took off to avoid dealing with the consequences he might face regarding the embezzlement of funds from clients and acquaintances. Prior to his departure, Ritchie sent letters to all of his clients and his spouse falsely describing a long-term history of drug and alcohol abuse. He believed that by sharing his alleged drug and alcohol addiction with his clients and wife, he would somehow not have to deal with the embezzlement and his gambling problem.

How would you proceed in treatment based on your clinical impressions?

_____

_____

A Window into the Past

Ritchie

Ritchie was born in a rural farm town in the Midwest where his parents were well known and respected. His parents emigrated from Sweden in the 1940s. Ritchie was raised in the Lutheran religion and attended services every Sunday. He is the eldest of three siblings and the only son. He was an all-American sports hero in his hometown, and everybody loved him. He was looked up to in his family and town as being a potential prominent leader in his community. As his father's only son, he was taught various sports and seemed to excel at most of them. His father coached him and showed off his talent to all of the townspeople. His mother saw him as second in command of the family. They clearly favored Ritchie over their daughters. Nonetheless, his sisters looked up to him because he protected them and stood up for them as their big brother, both in school and during extracurricular activities. Ritchie had no problem getting jobs during high school because everybody wanted him to work for them. There was, however, one blemish in Ritchie's high school career; this occurred around prom time. Ritchie's prom date was a popular young girl who had an appetite for drinking. She asked Ritchie to drive to a nearby mailbox to pick up a bottle of hard liquor that she had hidden. Prior to arriving at the prom, Ritchie saw a friend a few blocks away. He pulled over to talk to his buddy, and a policeman noticed he was in a "no standing" zone. The police officer leaned into the car to ask Ritchie to move the vehicle, and he noticed the open bottle of liquor on the seat. The next day on the front page of the local paper, Ritchie, the all-American high school teenager, was exposed as having a drinking problem. He was humiliated and never felt comfortable again in his hometown. Very few people left this farm town after graduating from high school; hence, the community was surprised when Ritchie elected to move out West and take a basketball scholarship in urban California.

Carmen

Carmen, Ritchie's wife, was born and raised in a large West Coast city. She is a Columbian American woman and the youngest of four girls. Her parents were born in Columbia. She lived a comfortable life in the United States and enjoyed relationships with her extended family, many of whom lived nearby. When Carmen was ten years old, her father was incarcerated for selling cocaine. She was shocked because her father was "her hero." He had a great sense of humor, was charming, and often took the family on vacations. She knew her father traveled and worked hard but never imagined that he was involved in illegal business. She eventually completed high school and received her degree in business at a local community college. She worked for her uncle as an administrative assistant in his computer software company, where she met Ritchie, who was a customer of her uncle.

Ritchie and Carmen

Ritchie and Carmen had a short courtship of one year and married soon thereafter. They had similar goals: to raise a family, enjoy the company of friends, and spend time together pursuing their interests of tennis and travel. Carmen continued to work part time for her uncle when Frank was born. She was close to Ritchie, yet she felt there was something going on in his life that she could not put her finger on. It wasn't until he admitted to his gambling problem that she was reminded of her father. She once again felt betrayed by the man in her life.

Carmen had difficulty with insomnia, flashbacks of her husband being gone, sadness, depression, and anger. She was encouraged to find and develop support systems through GamAnon and therapy to assist her with these issues. She joined a co-dependency group and learned to ask for emotional and physical support from her group members and other safe people in her life. Part of Carmen's therapy included learning to set appropriate boundaries with others in her life. Due to the financial devastation caused by Ritchie's gambling and living in a community property state, Carmen was encouraged by group members to file for a legal separation and ultimately divorce her husband. She divorced Ritchie while he was in prison and was able to cut any further financial liabilities related to his gambling. She was not, however, able to avoid all of the legal and financial consequences that occurred prior to her legal separation.

Frank

Frank is an eight year old bi-cultural boy who presents older than his stated age. He is close to both Carmen and Ritchie and has taken the role of the parentified child, where he tries to keep order in the family by nurturing Carmen, Ritchie, and Marco. He has done well in school and continues to excel both academically and athletically in his karate in spite of the recent developments between his parents.

Marco

Marco is a four year old bi-cultural boy. He is close to Carmen, looks up to his older brother Frank and often seeks out their affection and guidance. He started preschool part time eight months ago and recently clings to the teachers often leaving group activities with other children. He enjoys playing games and learning new skills, yet has difficulty making choices for himself. Recently the teachers report that Marco often asks, "Is it time to go home?"

- What are your clinical impressions regarding the Williamses?

  _____

  _____

- Based on your assessment, what interventions might you suggest for Frank and Marco?

  _____

  _____

Embracing the Essence

Session with Ritchie and Carmen

The therapist was impressed by how calmly and articulately Ritchie shared his story, especially knowing that he would potentially be incarcerated. He did not seem nervous at all. Although his words portrayed remorse, the tone of his voice did not. He did not present with the grandiosity of most gamblers. Carmen did not express any affect throughout the session.

> **THERAPIST:** I'm glad you came in today.
>
> **RITCHIE:** I don't know how I got to this point. I hope I can get my life back.
>
> **THERAPIST:** It seems to me that we first need to address your compulsive gambling.
>
> **RITCHIE:** What can I do?
>
> **THERAPIST:** Continuing with therapy, attending Gamblers Anonymous, and finding a sponsor is the first step. (Turns to look at Carmen, who has a blank look on her face.) Carmen, what's going on?
>
> **RITCHIE:** I made a mess of our lives; she must hate me.
>
> **THERAPIST:** Carmen, can you share what you are feeling right now?
>
> **CARMEN:** (Still looks blank.)
>
> **THERAPIST:** (Moves a little closer to Carmen.) Can you take a moment, close your eyes, and let yourself feel whatever you are aware of right now? Take your time, it's okay.
>
> **CARMEN:** (Sits for several minutes; a tear falls from her eye. She looks up and speaks softly.) I feel the same loss that I felt when my father went to prison.
>
> **THERAPIST:** (Puts her hand gently on Carmen's.) I hear your sadness.

- What are your thoughts about Ritchie?

  _____

  _____

- Describe how you might deal with Carmen.

  _____

  _____

- What would be your next step?

  _____

  _____

Exploratory Research and Resource Corner

- What resources would help you understand more about gambling?

_____

_____

- Describe what homework assignments or activities you might explore to help the Williamses.

_____

_____

Ritchie faced the consequences of his embezzlement and was sentenced to one year in prison with work furlough, which ultimately became work release. Following his release from prison, he was placed on intensive probation and is currently on standard probation, where he will remain until restitution has been made to all of his victims. Although the preliminary sentence was for 30 years, he served only one year. It appears that at the rate of payment of his restitution, Ritchie will be on standard probation for the rest of his life. Ritchie stayed involved in Gamblers Anonymous throughout his prison sentence but was denied his request to participate in therapy. Both prior to and during his incarceration, the therapist worked very closely with Carmen, Frank, and Marco to assist them in making the necessary emotional adjustments to dealing with life without Ritchie in their home.

- What are some of the issues that might be addressed in working with Frank and Marco?

_____

_____

- Describe the challenges Carmen and the boys may face while Ritchie is away.

_____

_____

THOUGHTS TO PONDER

"Intercultural couples can rightfully be considered a unique opportunity for therapists to crystallize what marriage therapy strives for: helping couples to have a fulfilling, gratifying, and rewarding relationship even in the face of seemingly insurmountable challenges." (Sullivan and Cottone, p. 224)

TAKE A ONE-MINUTE VACATION

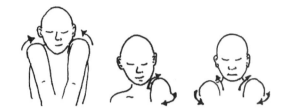

Shoulder Circles Slowly roll the right shoulder clockwise, squeezing it toward the ear, then down, forward, and up. Repeat several times. Reverse direction of circle and then repeat on opposite side.

Finally, rotate both shoulders at the same time; then repeat in the opposite direction.

Celebrating Family Culture

The Williamses are among thousands of families who have suffered the impact of compulsive gambling. In addition to the addiction, they also have been forced to change the structure of their life due to the incarceration of Ritchie. For Carmen, it's a repetition of her father's incarceration when she was ten. Both Frank and Marco have to deal with the mistrust and betrayal of a father they trusted. There are few services available for families of incarcerated men and women; in addition, families are reluctant to talk with others about their situation and if so, often deal with feelings of shame, that people will look down on them. The financial strains of Ritchie's gambling further placed the Williamses in a dramatic state of lifestyle change. Carmen became a single parent, and Frank and Marco are victims of Ritchie's addiction.

Park, Griffiths, and Irwing (2004) studied the personality traits in pathological gamblers. They found that competitiveness and lack of deferment of gratification were predictive of pathological gambling. "One could see how a competitive person would be attracted to gambling by the competitive and challenging nature of the behavior. However, why are competitive people at particular risk of developing pathological gambling behavior? It could be hypothesized that competitive gamblers are less inclined to 'throw the towel in' and/or accept a loss, and, as a result are more prone to chasing behavior.

Chasing behaviors is self-perpetuating; when gamblers chase losses, it is highly probable, they will lose more and the need to recoup losses increases as time passes." (Parks and Griffiths, 2004, p. 209)

Braman (2004) notes that since 1970 the incarceration rate in the United States has more than tripled. Comfort (2003) studied the experience of women visiting their incarcerated partners. She notes that erratic scheduling and prolonged waiting to see their partners suggests that women experience a form of secondary prisonization through their ongoing contact with the correctional system. Codd (2002) notes that the self-help groups for women conceal the real crises of the negative effects of rising rates of incarceration combined with a lack of services for prisoners' families. "There is a socially sanctioned expectation that women act as caregivers and self-help groups promote women's caring roles, [and] supporting such groups merely promotes the continuing transmission of oppressive gendered expectations" (Codd, 2002, p. 41). Edin, Nelson, and Paranal (2001) note that incarceration for fathers is often a powerful motivator to curb their destructive behavior so they can reconnect with their children.

Carmen's situation of being a Latina, being a single parent, and having a spouse in prison makes her a target for discrimination. Frank and Marco are bi-cultural and further face oppression being between two worlds of the Columbian Catholic and white Protestant culture while having to account for the absent, incarcerated father to friend and relatives.

In the case of the Williamses, the impact of Ritchie's gambling addiction and ultimate incarceration placed the family at risk for oppression, financial insecurity, loss of trust, and major adjustment psychologically and socially.

- Describe how Ritchie's gambling affected the lives of his family.

  _____

  _____

- As the therapist working with the Williamses, what clinical tools would help you maintain objectivity and connection?

  _____

  _____

THERAPIST'S TOOLS

Maintaining physical, psychological, and spiritual health is crucial for therapists not only for their personal and professional development, but also to ensure objectivity in the therapeutic relationship and to prevent burnout. Practicing yoga and meditation can influence a therapist's health in a positive way. Yoga is one of the six traditional systems of East Indian philosophy aimed at quieting the mind, enhancing spiritual growth, and nourishing the body. Valente and Marotta (2005) studied the impact of regular yoga practice in the personal and professional lives of psychotherapists. They found that the therapist's yoga practice influenced internal self-awareness, balance, and acceptance of self and others. The impulsive behavior that Ritchie is dealing with in his addiction and the self-esteem issues facing Carmen can be helped with yoga and meditation. Both the family and therapist benefit from being equipped with lifelong tools for maintaining balance.

Yoga. When practicing yoga, stretches several parts of the human body are engaged.

1. Consciously focusing on the breath facilitates a feeling of being centered and relaxed.
2. Moving our bodies in various yoga stretches expands the muscles, increases blood circulation, energizes and relaxes the body, and supplies the organs with a fresh supply of oxygen. The extraordinary benefits of a simple stretch can enhance the well-being of a therapist and client in the workplace and at home. Therapists can teach clients conscious breathing and stretches to relieve anxiety and increase energy, focus, and concentration.

Meditation. Therapists continually seek avenues to enhance objectivity in the therapeutic relationship. Many stimuli influence the therapeutic relationship; for example, unresolved issues, sensory stimuli, identification with the client, and sometimes just having a bad day. Therapists can gain insight through meditation practice.

Burnout. One cannot ignore the high incidence of burnout among helping professionals. Skovholt (2001) identifies "caring burnout" typically experienced by helping professionals. In addition to the needs of clients, therapists are dealing with organizational and political stressors such as lack of resources and shortage of staff. Chronic stress can lead to physical illness, disturbed sleep, poor eating habits, immune system resistance, and impaired performance. Yoga and meditation are two avenues that can increase a therapist's self-esteem, energy, and work performance, and these practices can be implemented in both formal and informal ways. Here are some suggestions.

1. At various points during the day, focus on your breathing.
2. Begin your day with one to five minutes of silent awareness and create a positive intention to set the stage for your day.
3. Check in with your body several times during the day and realize when you need a stretch, and do it.
4. Eat your lunch in an environment that permits you to let go of work talk.
5. In your workspace, keep plants, a small fountain, relaxing music, and other soothing objects that stimulate the senses.

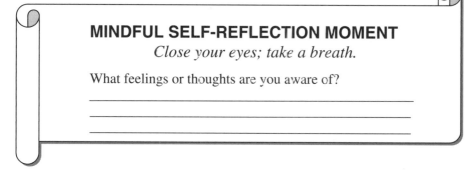

MINDFUL SELF-REFLECTION MOMENT
Close your eyes; take a breath.

What feelings or thoughts are you aware of?

Riding the Wave

Upon Ritchie's release, individual, marriage, and group counseling were resumed. Although Ritchie was invited to move back home and live with Carmen, his now ex-wife, and Frank and Marco, he was reluctant to move back. He had to process the loss of his marriage and adjust to living in a liberated environment, yet with the constraints of being on probation. He had continued work to do, recovery from compulsive gambling, and his victims continued to harass him and his family, although restitution was being made. Ritchie was also encouraged to develop a pressure-relief program. Pressure Relief is a program associated with Gamblers Anonymous and is designed to assist people in communicating with their creditors, reestablishing credit, and developing fiscally responsible practices. Because of Ritchie's accounting background, Pressure Relief was a good way for Ritchie to give back to the Gamblers Anonymous program.

There were several innovative tools used with Ritchie's family members and with Ritchie. While incarcerated, Ritchie was encouraged to practice deep breathing, journaling, and creative visualization. Carmen was encouraged to exercise, journal, and practice creative visualization to assist her in developing relaxation techniques. The therapist took the boys bowling at least twice a month and treated them individually and collectively, encouraging them to express their feelings and to learn to live with their new lifestyle and challenges.

- Describe your clinical impressions of the Williames at this point in treatment.

  _____

  _____

- What would be your next step in treatment?

  _____

TAKE A ONE-MINUTE VACATION

Neck Stretches Press head away from shoulders, gently tilting head backward so chin aims at ceiling. Then bring chin forward, pressing against the chest. Feel the back of the neck open and stretch. Bring head to center, tilting it to the left, lowering the ear toward the left shoulder. Turn head slightly to the side and slowly roll it back to center and then repeat on the right side. Feel the neck extend as you lean to each side. Remember to breathe throughout the stretch.

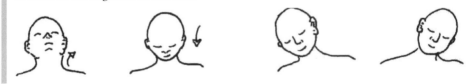

Beyond Treatment

Ritchie is continuing regular attendance in Gamblers Anonymous. Although Carmen has finished her co-dependency group, she meets with others from her group on a regular basis. She supports others in similar circumstances, and socializes with friends she has made in her recovery group. Ritchie is a sponsor to other Gamblers Anonymous members in early recovery. He has set a limit of sponsoring only three people at a time and has chosen people in the Gamblers Anonymous program who are eager and ready to work. He has become a teacher and trainer for Pressure Relief. Ritchie and Carmen have become active in a nondenominational church, working with other couples undergoing marital stress. Both Ritchie and Carmen have shared with Frank and Marcos the reasons for their divorce and continued commitment to their family. They speak openly to them about compulsive gambling and addictions in general. Ritchie has interacted with both of the boys in areas of their interest.

- What strengths does Ritchie present? Carmen?

_____

_____

- What services might Frank and Marco benefit from?

_____

_____

MINDFUL SELF-REFLECTION MOMENT
Close your eyes; take a breath.

What feelings or thoughts are you aware of?

_____

_____

_____

REFERENCES

Braman, D. (2004). *Doing time on the outside: Incarceration and family life in urban America.* Ann Arbor, MI: University of Michigan Press.

Codd, H. (2002). "The ties that bind": Feminist perspectives on self-help groups for prisoner's partners. *Howard Journal of Criminal Justice, 41*(4), 334–347.

Comfort, M. L. (2003). In the tube at San Quentin: The secondary prisonization of women visiting inmates. *Journal of Contemporary Ethnography. 32*(1), 77–107.

Edin, K., Nelson, T. J., & Paranal, R. (2001). *Fatherhood and incarceration as potential turning points in the criminal careers of unskilled men.* Evanston, IL: Northwestern University Press.

Parke, A., Griffiths, M., Irwing, P. (2004). Personality traits in pathological gambling: sensation seeking, deferment of gratification and competitiveness as risk factors. *Addiction Research and Theory, 12*(3) 201–212.

Rittenhouse, J. (2000). Using eye movement desentization and reprocessing to treat complex PTSD in a biracial client. *Cultural diversity and Ethnic Minority Psychology* 6(4) 399–408.

Skovholt, T. M. (2001). *The resilient practitioner: Burnout prevention and self-care strategies for counselors, therapists, teachers, and health professionals.* Needham Heights, MA: Allyn & Bacon.

Sullivan, C. & Cottone, R. R. (2006). Culturally based couple therapy and intercultural relationships: a review of the literature. *The family Journal: counseling and therapy for couples and families 14*(3) 221–225.

Suzuki-Crumly, J. & Hyers, L. L. (2004). The relationship among ethnic identity, psychological well-being, and intergroup competence: An investigation of two biracial groups *Cultural diversity and Ethnic Minority Psychology 10* (2) 137–150.

Valente, V., & Marotta, A. (2005). The impact of yoga on the professional and personal life of the psychotherapist. *Contemporary Family Therapy, 27*(1), 65–80.

SUGGESTED READING

Baum, N. (2004). Coping with "absence-presence": Noncustodial fathers' parenting behaviors. *American Journal of Orthopsychiatry, 74*(3), 316–324.

Cooper, P. C. (1999). Buddhist meditation and countertransference: A case study. *The American Journal of Psychoanalysis, 56*(1), 71–85.

Finger, W., & Arnold, E. M. (2002). Mind-body interventions: Applications for social work practice. *Social Work Health Care, 35*(4), 57–78.

Heineman, M. (2001). Dynamics in the compulsive gambler's relationships. In (Ed.), *Losing your shirt* (pp. 21–33). CompCare Publishers, MI,

Johnson, E. I., & Waldfogel, J. (2002). Parental incarceration: Recent trends and implications for child welfare. *Social Service Review, 76*(3), 460–479.

Klein, S. R., Bartholomew-Geannina, S., & Hibbert, J. (2002). Inmate family functioning. *International Journal of Offender therapy and Comparative Criminology, 46*(1), 95–111.

Martin, J. S. (2001). *Inside looking out: Jailed fathers' perceptions about separation from children.* New York: Scholarly Publishing, LLC.

Petersilia, J. (2001). When prisoners return to communities: Political, economic and social consequences. *Federal Probation, 65*(1), 3–8.

Protinsky, H., & Coward, L. (2001). Developmental lessons of seasoned marital and family therapists: A qualitative investigation. *Journal of Marital and Family Therapy, 27*(3), 375–384.

Ricketts, T., & McCaskill, A. (2004). Differentiating normal and problem gambling: A grounded theory approach. *Addiction Research and Theory, 12*(1), 77–87.

Rose, D. R., Cear, T. R., & Ryder, J. A. (2001). Addressing the unintended consequences of incarceration through community-oriented services at the neighborhood level. *Corrections Management Quarterly, 5*(3), 62–71.

6 Multigenerational Abuse: The Story of the Santiagos

While laughing with your child, you'll take a peak at heaven.
Ford, 1995

Getting Started

> "This violence has to stop! My father abused my mother; my husband abused me; and now my son Juan is beating on my mother and me. What is wrong with the men in our family? Will it ever stop; will this cycle go on forever?"

What reactions are you aware of right now?

_____

_____

Juan is a tall, handsome, thirteen-year-old Hispanic boy. He has become aggressive, angry, and violent over the last year. The Santiagos were referred to the La Luna Community Mental Health Clinic due an incident between Juan and his mother. Juan was yelling at his mother and started hitting her with closed fists. His mother Juanita pushed him away; he fell backward and hit his head on a dining room chair. Juan sustained a small bruise. The bruise was identified by a teacher at school, who reported it to Child Protective Services. A Child Protective Services investigator made the referral to the La Luna Clinic upon finding that the current parent-child conflict was not abuse but could lead to an abusive situation. The Santiagos were referred to address the problem before an incident occurred that required the removal of the children from the Santiagos' home.

• What do you know about the cycle of abuse?

_____

_____

• What might Juanita be experiencing?

_____

_____

• What would be your next step?

_____

_____

THOUGHTS TO PONDER

"Twenty-two to thirty-seven percent of Emergency Room visits made by women are for injuries sustained from relationships and seventy-five percent of the women will be revictimized. Women who are abused suffer from depression, anxiety, phobias and forty-five to eighty-five percent of those women suffer from Post Traumatic Stress Disorder (PTSD)." (Murdaugh, Hung, Sowell, and Santang, 2004, p. 107)

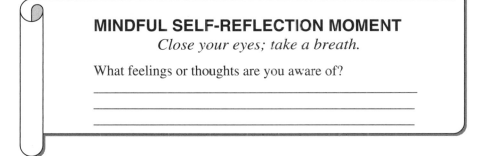

MINDFUL SELF-REFLECTION MOMENT
Close your eyes; take a breath.

What feelings or thoughts are you aware of?

_____

_____

_____

A Window into the Past

Juanita

Juanita is a petite, thirty-three-year-old, Mexican-born woman who grew up in a large family. Her father and grandfather suffered from alcoholism. She moved to Los Angeles with her family when she was ten years old. Learning English was difficult for Juanita, completing high school was a challenge. Juanita wanted to continue her education, but her parents felt that she should marry, raise a family, and stay at home. She remembers her mother telling Juanita and her six siblings to be quiet when her father returned home from work and not to aggravate him so he would not be verbally abusive toward them. His alcoholism affected everyone in the family. Her father physically abused her mother. Juanita resented her mother for exposing her to this type of violence. Juanita claims this is the reason she left her husband Pedro. She currently works at a local fast food restaurant, yet she still dreams of becoming an interior decorator and recalls with fond memories reading decorating magazines and being the person in the family everyone came to when they decorated their home.

Pedro

Pedro, thirty-five years old, also Mexican born, was a migrant farm worker. He moved to Los Angeles when he was twenty years old, completed high school, and studied business education at a local career center. Pedro wanted to achieve financial success, yet he felt restrained as an immigrant Latino man. He reported incidents in which he felt disrespected and was passed over for employment opportunities despite his qualifications. He was experienced in mathematics and had an intuitive knack for business. When asked about Pedro, Juanita is unwilling to discuss him, yet Juan has mentioned on several occasions that "she" kicked Pedro out. Juan reported that "she" kicked his father out because he wasn't being very "nice" or "good" and was a "problem."

Juanita and Pedro

Juanita and Pedro met through mutual friends and were married when Juanita was nineteen years old. She was excited about getting married, and leaving her parents' house, and she hoped to have a life of fun and adventure. Pedro was charming and took her out dining and dancing, which gave Juanita another view of socializing and independence.

Juanita came home from work one day and found her husband in their bedroom with another woman. Despite this devastating incident, she stayed with him, yet he continued to sleep with other women. Being a devout Catholic, Juanita did not want to divorce, but she was also ashamed of what was happening in the marriage. Their relationship, though "never perfect," began to turn into angry, "hurtful" arguments. Juanita states that "we barely even talked," and not too long after Franco was born was the first time during an argument that Pedro hit her. She stated that this happened several times over the next year before she finally threw Pedro out of the house. Currently Pedro has no contact with either Juan or Franco, Juan's younger brother. According to Juanita, the last she heard Pedro was on the East Coast somewhere with his "girlfriend."

Juan

Juanita reports that until recently Juan was the perfect little boy. She stated that he has met all developmental milestones. He had been a good student, active in after-school activities such as cub scouts, and involved at their church. She did mention that she noted some jealousy from Juan when Franco was born, but she felt this was normal. Juan had no history of being argumentative with authority or getting into fights before this past year.

Juan is in the seventh grade. This incident with his mother was the first time he had hit her, but prior anger outbursts have included punching the wall, yelling and screaming, and calling his mother derogatory names. Juanita reports that these outbursts occur when she tells Juan to do something such as clean the dishes or his room, do his homework, or go to bed. The incident mentioned previously occurred after Juanita told Juan to clean his room before playing Nintendo.

In the past month Juan has gotten into fights on the playground at school and cursed at the teacher's aid in his classroom. Juanita reports no aggression toward his younger brother Franco. Juanita states that these behaviors emerged not long after she kicked Juan's father, Pedro, out of the house. In the last week Juanita had plans to go out on a date, and Juan hid her car keys so she had to cancel the date.

Franco

Franco is six years old. He is the light of Juanita's life. He looks like her favorite brother and is a charming and engaging child. Juanita enjoys spending time with him and focuses her energy on doing activities with him on her days off. Belinda, Juanita's mother, takes care of him after school. Franco admires his older brother Juan.

Belinda (Maternal Grandmother)

Belinda was born and raised in Mexico. She moved to the United States when she was twenty-five years old. She never worked outside the home, and her husband did not allow her to socialize with friends unless accompanied by either himself or a relative. She was busy raising seven children and was involved in their lives, making sure their needs were met. She is a warm and affectionate woman who was often the confidante of the local women in her community. Belinda was active in the Catholic Church, joined a Spanish-speaking women's Bible group, and baked for many events held at the church. Although she suffered the pains of her husband's physical abuse and alcoholism, she rarely complained. Her husband died five years ago and Belinda moved in with Juanita. She is financially dependent on her children, particularly Juanita. Recently she developed diabetes and has become depressed. She does not live close enough to her local church to walk to her Bible study class and feels overwhelmed with the responsibility of caring for Juan and Franco. She's reluctant to ask Juanita to take her to church because she knows how tired Juanita is when she comes home from work.

- How have traditional values impacted the Santiagos?

_____

_____

- Describe the cultural implications that might account for Pedro's behavior.

_____

_____

Embracing the Essence

There are several key initial impressions. Juan states that he hates his mom and is unwilling to discuss his father. He reports that his grandmother Belinda sides with Juanita and she makes him angry because he feels that Juanita and Belinda gang up on him. He admits to pushing his grandmother on several occasions and feels bad about it, yet his anger gets the best of him. He feels that Franco gets all of their love and is seen as the "special angel" and he is the "bad seed." Juan is initially resistant to being in therapy and reports that "she" made me come. Currently Juan perceives that he is seeing a therapist because he is "bad." He often expresses a wish to be seen as a "good boy" by his mother.

The therapist made some observations: (1) Juanita does not say a single positive thing about Juan; (2) Juanita seems to be focusing all of her attention on the younger brother Franco; and (3) Juan has a strong resentment toward his mother possibly related to his father leaving. After the first session Juanita was so focused on Juan being bad that the therapist wasn't sure how to work with her. Juan appeared to have self-esteem issues and anger and resentments that were projected onto his mother.

First Session with Juanita, Juan, and Therapist

THERAPIST: What brings you here today?

JUANITA: (She begins speaking very rapidly.) Well, my son Juan is a big pain in the ass. And if he keeps it up I will lose my kids. His attitude I can do without, but his little brother needs him.

JUAN: Screw you . . . (Juan mumbles under his breath.)

JUANITA: (Pauses and sighs.) See what I mean; he is constantly arguing and fighting with me. He has hit me. And recently when he was hitting me I pushed him away. CPS [Child Protective Services] referred me here. I don't know what to do with him. I can't control him. He has been a holy terror since his father left . . . he's even pushed my mother, an elderly woman, when she tried to discipline him. Where's the respect!?

JUAN: When you kicked him out. Bitch . . . (Juan again mumbles under his breath.)

JUANITA: All of this wouldn't be happening if I had a man in my life. Then he would have an authority figure that could keep him in line. I don't know what to do anymore. (Loud sigh.) I just don't know what to do. (Tearful sniffle.) What can I do? How can I keep from losing them. . .? From losing Franco [Juan's younger brother]? He is just so sweet. (She gestures to Franco, who has been gleefully playing on the floor with a toy truck.) I remember when you used to be this sweet and you listened to me. (She speaks to Juan.) What is wrong with you? You're just like your father.

JUAN: Whatever. . .

THERAPIST: Juan, I have heard what your mom sees is going on in the family; what do you think is going on?

JUAN: Huh I don't know . . . (He mumbles.)

JUANITA: See what I mean, he is being disrespectful. (To Juan.) Stop being disrespectful; answer the man and look at people when you speak to them.

THERAPIST: This is just a thought; maybe I could meet with Juan alone and get his picture of what is going on?

JUANITA: Sure, whatever it takes . . . (To Juan.) Now you behave. Let's go, Franco. Can I take this toy. . .? (Door closes.)

• What are your thoughts about Juanita's feelings toward Juan?

_____

_____

• How would you address the abuse with Juan's grandmother Belinda?

_____

_____

- What are your clinical impressions?

_____

_____

- What more do you need to know?

_____

_____

THOUGHTS TO PONDER

"A study of Latino youth found four themes regarding parental and school attitudes that contributed to their educational success.

1. *Parental emphasis on the importance of education.* This consisted verbal support for all educational matters.
2. *Parents' support of children's autonomy.* Parents, although not directly involved in school matters, conveyed enormous trust in their children and allowed them to do what they felt was in their best interest.
3. *Nonverbal support for educational endeavors.* Through their behavior parents showed support and valued their children's efforts.
4. *Faculty role models and mentors.* Students mentioned at least one teacher when asked to name the three most influential people during their high school years. Their teachers took an interest in both their personal and academic lives." (Adapted from Ceballo, 2004, pp. 176–183)

TAKE A ONE-MINUTE VACATION

Shining Skull Breath The shining skull breath is an excellent practice to begin the day or restore energy when you are tired or need to feel refreshed. It is a breathing practice to cleanse and purify. The spinal fluid changes pressure according to the rhythms of normal respiration and gets a big shift in pressure when you have fast and forceful exhalation. Let's begin.

1. *Get comfortable; sit with your back straight and chest lifted.* Put your hands on your belly. Slowly and naturally take the breath in through your nose. Let your belly fill with air like a balloon.
2. *Quickly breathe out (this is the important part) and exhale forcefully through your nose.* Notice the inhalation is spontaneous; the exhalation is focused and forceful.

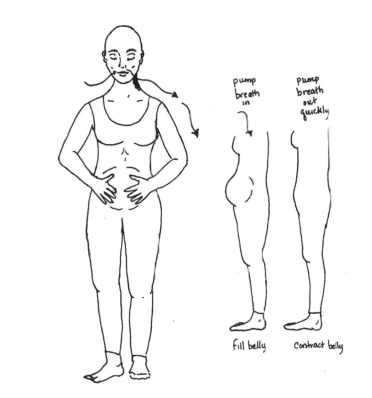

3. *Notice your own rhythm, slowly taking breath in and quickly and forcefully pumping it out by contracting the belly muscles.* There is a slight pause after each exhalation. And then begin again. Once you feel comfortable with the forceful exhalation, the pumping of your belly, and passive inhalation, slowly pick up the pace according to your own rhythm.

Fifth Session with Juan, Juanita, and Therapist

Prior to meeting with Juan, the therapist checked in with Juanita on how things were going. Each week Juanita would complain endlessly about how "bad Juan was this week." Meanwhile, Juan reported that he was working on his anger management, but Juanita wasn't any "nicer" to him. During the second, third, and fourth sessions Juan was given the assignment to do three positive things that would shock his mother. The therapist asked her to come in to get her reports on Juan's behavior.

THERAPIST: So how have things been going with you and Juan?

JUANITA: The day after your last session he got up from the dinner table and did all the dishes without even being asked. I was like, what has gotten into this kid? But I just sat there quietly. Later I thanked him for doing that and I took him and Franco for ice cream because he was so good. But that is not the only thing; I mean a few days later or something he picked flowers for me. I can't believe it, he picked flowers for me! That same day he mowed the lawn on the weekend without being asked. He was all of a sudden doing chores without being asked. He made his bed before going to school three times this week. I just don't know what has gotten into him. I was curious how things were going at school, so I asked Juan how school was going and he said "oh fine." So I asked his teacher. The teacher said that he has been fine and has not gotten into any fights in the last month, and all his homework has been turned in on time.

THERAPIST: Great! Would you mind if I have Juan come in here so he can hear your thoughts about how great he is doing?

JUANITA: Sure.

Therapist calls Juan in and asks Juanita to repeat what she had reported in the session.

JUANITA: (Repeats her report.)

JUAN: (Smiles and giggles.)

JUANITA: Okay, what is going on?

JUAN: I was supposed to do three different things . . . (He sheepishly smiles and laughs.) I would be so good it would surprise you. First I did the dishes; that was the number 1 different thing. Then I mowed the lawn without being asked, and that was number 2. And then number 3 was making my bed more often, but the other stuff I didn't even try to do . . . (Blushes.)

THERAPIST: So you can do "good" stuff without even trying?

JUAN: Yeah, I can. (Smiles.)

JUANITA: He is a good kid. So you gave me flowers and it wasn't even an assignment?

JUAN: I thought they were pretty and you like pink. . . . I know you like pink . . . so I picked them.

(The therapist asked Juan and his mother to rate their relationship on a 1–10 scale, and they both gave it a 6. In a later session they progressed to an 8.5.)

- Describe the dynamics that occurred between Juan and Juanita.

_____

_____

• What are the developmental issues facing Juan at 13 years old and Franco at 6 years old?

_____

_____

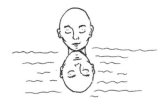

MINDFUL SELF-REFLECTION MOMENT
Close your eyes; take a breath.

What feelings or thoughts are you aware of?

_____

_____

_____

THERAPIST'S TOOLS

Consider the issues of boundaries in working with the Santiagos. Boundaries help us decide what actions and thoughts will move us toward what feels good and away from what does not feel good. "Personal boundaries are our psychological and interpersonal immune system" (Whitehead, 1994, p. 1). The history of abuse experienced by the Santiagos lends itself to generations of boundary distortion. A common coping mechanism to deal with the pain of being violated is to move into a state of numbness—avoiding feeling; this avoidance of feeling applies to all feelings, both good and bad, and is a needed defense to survive the abuse. Unfortunately, Juanita and Belinda do not have healthy tools to respond when they are violated and again find themselves in a perpetual cycle of abuse. Juan and Franco have experienced verbal abuse. How can you as the therapist help the Santiagos establish healthy boundaries? Explore the following tools:

1. *Detection.* Notice what's happening now.
2. *Action.* Make a decision about how you will deal with the situation (feeling, body, nutrition, behavior, thoughts) that confronts you now.

3. *Control.* You have dealt with the situation and feel satisfied with the outcome.
4. *Equilibrium.* Move on—your no longer are stuck in the feeling of the situation. (Whitehead, 1994)

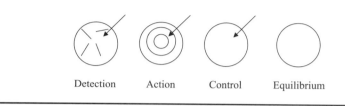

Detection   Action   Control   Equilibrium

Celebrating Family Culture

Mexicans are the largest Latino group in the United States; six out of ten Latinos have Mexican origins. Zinn and Wells (2000) note that the Mexican population tripled in size from approximately 4.5 million in 1970 to 13.5 million in 1990. In 2004 there were over eight million Mexican immigrants living in the US and the number is predicted to rise to over nine and a half million by 2010. (http://en.wikipedia.org/wiki/Immigration_to_the_United_States) Although Mexicans as a group have low family incomes and low educational completion, they have the largest average household size of all Latino groups. They maintain a large labor force, and women are an increasing segment of that labor force. In Mexico, men hold the position of patriarch in most family decisions, but there is a trend toward shared decision making because of acculturation of U.S. culture.

The Santiagos are confronted with many challenges that are related to acculturation and oppression and relevant to their traditional family values. The cycle of abuse is a core issue in treatment. Flores, Tschann, Marin, and Pantoja (2004) examined the relationship between acculturation and marital conflict among Mexican American couples. They found that more acculturated husbands and wives communicate their conflicts more directly than less acculturated husbands and wives. Field, Caetano, and Nelson (2004) found that the expectation of aggressive behavior following alcohol consumption appeared to be the most influential predictor for intimate partner violence. They also found that approval of marital aggression and aggressive expectations resulting from alcohol consumption are less common in whites than for blacks and Hispanics (p. 252).

Feerick and Haugaard (1999) found that witnessing marital violence was associated with other family mental health risks, and women who witnessed marital violence reported more symptoms of posttraumatic stress disorder. Murdaug, Hunt, Sowell, and Santana (2004) found that three-quarters of the Hispanic women they studied in the southeastern United States experienced physical violence within the year of the study. Most of those women were undocumented immigrants (95 percent), had little formal education beyond elementary school, were monolingual Spanish, and had low-paying jobs. Hispanic women are a vulnerable population, which places them at a disadvantage to leave abusive relationships and seek support. It is also important to note that divorce is frowned upon by the Catholic Church. Women who leave their husbands are looked upon with shame, and those who seek divorce are not encouraged to receive the sacraments in the church. Juanita and Belinda faced challenges that kept them stuck in the cycle of violence.

Bracero (1998) states that "Latino cultures have relatively rigid sex role expectations and norms that privilege men at the expense of women" (p. 264). Both Juanita and Belinda were victims of oppression within their own family. As an elder, Belinda is still experiencing abuse, now from her grandson, Juan, who follows the cycle of generational abuse.

Juan, a young Mexican, has not been unscathed by acculturation and his family challenges. Romero and Roberts (2003) studied stress and Mexican adolescents and found that youths of Mexican descent experienced stress related to their dual cultural and linguistic contexts. These bicultural youth experienced more depressive symptoms regardless of individual differences in demographics and self-esteem. The stress experienced by these youth was related to family obligations or derogatory ethnic jokes (p. 179).

Feerick and Haugaard (1999) discuss the situation of juvenile offenders who witness marital violence. Those youth who witness marital violence experience short- and long-term psychological problems, including aggression and violent behavior. Studies have found that adults exposed to marital violence as children experience higher levels of aggression, partner violence, and psychological distress than adults who did not witness marital violence. Juan is faced with losing his father, feeling rejected by his mother and grandmother, and trying to fit into a cultural that often does not support him. The Santiagos present with challenges that are intergenerational and cultural.

- Describe how culture has impacted the Santiagos' lives.

_____

_____

- What issues of oppression do the Santiagos face?

_____

_____

Riding the Wave

During the fifth through twelfth sessions with Juan and Juanita, the therapist tried to engage them in the following empowerment-building tasks.

Directed play therapy. In the second, third and fourth session the therapist worked alone with Juan. Juan and the therapist play the feelings card game, in which each player chose a card that asked to give a feeling response to a statement, and the mancala African stone game, where players move rocks around the board trying to get as many into their own home as possible to beat their opponent. The point of the game is to be the one who ends up with the most stones in their Mancala. In sessions five through twelve, Juan, the therapist and Juanita played both games with Juan teaching his mother how to play. Juanita bought the mancala game to play at home with Juan.

Anger management techniques. The therapist worked with Juan on basic anger management skills: for example, stop and think exercises, relaxation, counting to ten, and alternative means of releasing tension (i.e., through activities and sports).

Parenting classes. Juanita was referred to a parenting class to help her set boundaries and limits.

Exploratory Research and Resource Corner

- What teamwork activities might you explore to keep Juanita and Juan engaged in positive interactions?

_____

_____

Beyond Treatment

The Santiagos are on the road to recovery, yet will need much support along the way. Juanita and Belinda are discussing ways to transport Belinda to her women's Bible studies, where she meets with her friends during the study and afterward for coffee. Juan has offered to escort Belinda. The church has a youth program, and the family is discussing participation for Juan and possibly Franco. Juanita has discussed job training with the child protective worker to enable her to better support her family. The worker is trying to locate Pedro to solicit his financial support of the family. Juanita has joined a yoga class to help her cope with stress. She feels more relaxed when she comes home from work.

- How would you support the Santiagos at this point?

_____

_____

THOUGHTS TO PONDER

Twelve themes describe the process of leaving abusive relationships and maintaining positive change.

1. Acknowledging the truth/reality of the abusive relationship
2. Being receptive to and acting as an advocating voice
3. Accepting the support of others
4. Making adjustments to a new way of living
5. Acknowledging anger and feelings of loss/fear
6. Letting go of/releasing unproductive behaviors
7. Awakening/discovery of self
8. Looking within/focusing on self
9. Reconnecting with strengthening supportive relationships
10. Reaffirming faith-based beliefs and practices
11. Helping others/reaching out
12. Embracing a new perspective of self, others, life

Adapted from Senter and Caldwell (2002, pp. 547–561)

MINDFUL SELF-REFLECTION MOMENT
Close your eyes; take a breath.

What feelings or thoughts are you aware of?

_____

_____

_____

REFERENCES

Bracero, W. (1998). Intimidades: Confianza, gender, and hierarchy in the construction of Latino-Latina therapeutic relationships. *Cultural Diversity and Ethnic Minority Psychology, 4*(4), 264–277.

Ceballo, R. (2004). From barrios to Yale: The role of parenting strategies in families. *Hispanic Journal of Behavioral Sciences, 26*(2), 171–186.

Feerick, M. M., & Haugaard, J. J. (1999). Long-term effects of witnessing marital violence for women: The contribution of childhood physical and sexual abuse. *Journal of Family Violence, 14*(4), 377–398.

Field, C. A., Caetano, R., & Nelson, S. (2004). Alcohol and violence related cognitive risk factors associated with the perpetration of intimate partner violence. *Journal of Family Violence, 19*(4), 249–253.

Flores, E., Tschann, J. M., Marin, B. V., & Pantoja, P. (2004). Marital conflict and acculturation among Mexican American husbands and wives. *Cultural Diversity and Ethnic Minority Psychology, 10*(1), 39–52.

Ford, J. (1995) *Wonderful ways to love a child.* Berkeley, CA: Conari Press.

Romero, A. J., & Roberts, R. E. (2003). Stress within a bicultural context for adolescents of descent. *Cultural Diversity and Ethnic Minority Psychology, 9*(2), 171–184.

Schneider, M. G. (2004). The intersection of mental and physical health in older Mexican Americans. *Hispanic Journal of Behavioral Sciences, 26*(3), 333–355.

Senter, K. E., & Caldwell, C. (2002). Spirituality and the maintenance of change: A phenomenological study of women who leave abusive relationships. *Contemporary Family Therapy, 24*(4), 543–564.

Whitehead, T. (1995). Boundaries and Psychotherapy Part II: Healing damaged boundaries. Hakomi Journal, Fall Issue 11

Zinn, M. B., & Wells, B. (2000). Diversity within Latino Families: New lessons for family social science. In D. H. Damo, K. R. Allen, & M. A. Fine (Eds.), *Handbook of family diversity* (pp. 252–273). New York: Oxford University Press.

SUGGESTED READING

Baer, J. C., Prince, J. D., & Velez, J. (2004). Fusion or familialism: A construct problem in studies of Mexican American Adolescents. *Hispanic Journal of Behavioral Science, 26*(3), 263–273.

Buchbinder, E., & Eiskovitz, Z. (2003). Battered women's entrapment in shame: A phenomenological study. *American Journal of Orthopsychiatry, 73*(4), 355–366.

Butell, F. P., & Carney, M. M. (2004). A multidimensional assessment of a batterer treatment program: An alert to a problem? *Research on Social Work Practice, 14*(2), 93–101.

Chiriboga, D. A. (2004). Some thoughts on the measurement of acculturation among Mexican American elders. *Hispanic Journal of Behavioral Sciences, 26*(3), 274–292.

De Anda, R. M. (2005). Employment hardship among Mexican-Origin Women. *Hispanic Journal of Behavioral Sciences, 27*(1), 43–59.

Eby, K. K. (2004). Exploring the stressors of low-income women with abusive partners: Understanding their needs and developing effective community responses. *Journal of family Violence, 19*(4), 221–232.

El-Khoury, M. Y., Dutton, M. A., Goodman, L. A., Engel, L., Belamaric, R. J., & Murphy, M. (2004). Ethnic differences in battered women's formal help-seeking strategies: A focus on health, mental health and spirituality. *Cultural Diversity and Ethnic Minority Psychology, 10*(4), 383–393.

Felix-Ortiz, M., Villatoro-Velazquez, J. A., Medina-Mora, M. E., & Newcomb, M. D. (2001). Adolescent drug use in Mexico and among Mexican American adolescents in the United

States: Environmental influences and individual characteristics. *Cultural Diversity and Ethnic Minority Psychology, 7*(1), 27–46

Hyman, M. (2004). Paradigm shift: The end of "normal science." In Medicine: Understanding Function in Nutrition, Health, and Disease. *Alternative Therapies in Health and Medicine, 10*(4), 10–15, 90–93.

Murdaugh, C., Hunt, S., Sowell, R., & Santana, I. (2004). Domestic violence in Hispanics in the Southeastern United States: A survey and needs analysis. *Journal of Family Violence, 19*(2), 107–115.

Ronan, G. F., Dreer, L. E., Dollard, K. M., & Ronan, D. W. (2004). Violent couples: Coping and communication skills. *Journal of Family Violence, 19*(7), 131–137.

Scott, K. L. (2004). Stage of change as a predictor of attrition among men in a batterer treatment program. *Journal of Family Violence, 19*(1), 37–47.

Waldrop, A. E., & Resick, P. A. (2004). Coping among adult female victims of domestic violence. *Journal of Family Violence, 19*(5), 291–302.

7 The Heartfelt Dad: The Story of the Chens

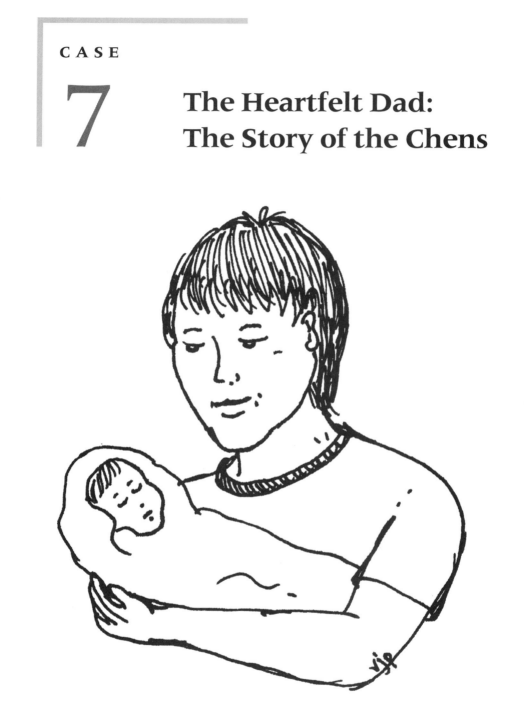

*Intimacy requires that you release yourself to the moment
and stand before the golden door of truth.*
Rodegast & Stanton, 1989, p. 81

Getting Started

"I'm terrified! My wife is in the hospital and might die. I need to care for our new born baby Sean. He's six weeks old. Can I do this alone?"

What reactions are you aware of right now?

_____

_____

Danny is a twenty-six-year-old Chinese American and a new dad. He was referred to the Family Crisis Center by his son's pediatrician, who reported that Danny is experiencing anxiety. Danny's wife Leilani recently gave birth to their first child, Sean, six weeks ago. Last week Leilani was in a serious automobile accident and incurred a brain injury. She will be in the hospital for two months. At present, she is in critical care. Danny has taken time off from work to care for Sean.

- What questions might you ask Danny during this first interview?

_____

_____

- What services might Danny need at this time?

_____

_____

A Window into the Past

Danny

Danny is a twenty-six-year-old Chinese American man born and raised in California. He is the younger of two children; his brother, Randy, is twenty-eight years old. His father, Alan, is a computer programmer for a large national corporation. His mother, Ann, is an attorney and works for a local law firm. Danny's grandparents, both school teachers, live several hours away. Danny attended a public high school in an upper-middle-class community and enjoyed a comfortable lifestyle. He studied Tai Kwan Do and competed nationally, and he was a gifted writer. He attended college in California and is currently a journalist for a local newspaper. Danny likes to travel, enjoys socializing, and has many friends from high school and college.

Danny describes his father as the "head of the house" and his mother as a warm and easy-going person. His brother, Randy, is an accountant. Danny, his parents, and his brother have a cordial relationship and do not share common interests other than family. Danny has several cousins who lived nearby while he was growing up. They visited each other often yet kept separate lives. Danny dated while in high school and college and in college was introduced to Leilani by a friend in college.

Leilani

Leilani is a twenty-four-year-old Chinese American woman born and raised in California. She is the middle child of six children and has two older sisters, ages twenty-six and twenty-eight, and three younger brothers, ages twenty-three, twenty, and nineteen. Her family is traditional in the sense that her maternal grandparents live in the house with her parents and siblings. Her mother, Jasmine, and father, George, have large families and each has four siblings. Leilani's father owns a local restaurant, and all of the employees are members of the family.

Both Jasmine and George's family live in the same community. The family has an "open door" policy in which family members visit unannounced and are involved in each other's private lives, frequently offering opinions and advice. Jasmine felt obligated to take advice from family members before making decisions regarding events in her life. Although she disagreed at times, she usually went along to avoid tension and disrespect toward family elders.

Leilani attended a local high school. She has artistic talents and won several awards in high school for her paintings. She studied art in college and met Danny during her sophomore year. She dated him almost exclusively with the exception of a few casual dates. Leilani secured a job with an advertising company as an artist.

- Describe the nature of Leilani's family relationships?

  _____

  _____

- Describe the nature of Danny's family relationships?

  _____

  _____

Danny and Leilani

Danny and Leilani married one year after graduating from college. They enjoyed each other's company, planned their future, and spent time with friends.

Danny loved to travel and spent many hours imagining the exotic places he and Leilani would visit together. Although Leilani enjoyed new adventures, she did not feel the need to travel as much as Danny. She felt that Danny was at times unrealistic when he shared his thoughts about traveling with their children.

Danny liked to sit down and talk about his feelings and daily activities, yet sometimes he felt that Leilani was too busy "running around" doing things for her extended family. He felt left out and frustrated. He felt intruded upon by Leilani's family when they made plans without consulting him and assumed that he would be interested in the many family events, which occurred almost every weekend. He wanted more time alone with Leilani. After one year of marriage, Leilani became pregnant with Sean. She worked at the advertising company until her eighth month of pregnancy. She had a normal delivery, and Sean was in good health.

- Describe your impressions of Danny and Leilani.

  _____

  _____

- Describe the strengths inherent in the Chens.

  _____

  _____

MINDFUL SELF-REFLECTION MOMENT
Close your eyes; take a breath.

What feelings or thoughts are you aware of?

_____

_____

_____

Embracing the Essence

"If they don't leave me alone, I'm going to scream!"

Leilani was visiting her parents one weekend and had left Sean with her cousin Rebecca. While she was driving home, she was critically injured in an automobile accident. Although she and Danny often fought about her driving too fast, the accident was not her fault. The driver of the other car was taking prescription medication that altered his perception and his car went out of control.

Leilani was in intensive care, and the extent of her brain damage was unknown. She regained consciousness after a week. The family was told that she would not come home for at least two months. Danny stayed at home with Sean and visited Leilani in the hospital while Leilani's mother cared for Sean. Although Danny was grateful for the help, he felt intruded upon by the constant comings and goings of Leilani's family. He needed time to process his feelings and thoughts. Leilani's family visited the house without calling and chose to sleep over without an invitation, and they offered advice about how to care for Sean. Danny needed private time with Sean and was relishing the bonding that was taking place with his newborn son. He wondered how the accident would affect Leilani. He needed time to think.

- Describe how you would proceed clinically with Danny?

  _____

  _____

- What do you need to know?

  _____

THOUGHTS TO PONDER

"The novice enters practice as a new canoeist enters white water—with anxiety, some instruction, a crude map, and some previous life experience. All of a sudden, for example, there is the client in front of the counselor, telling a very personal, real story. The story often comes in a complex ambiguity form. The experience is like the sudden rush of water, rocks, and rapids demanding instant understanding and reaction. The novice often has the urge both to call 911 and appear calm, collected, and professional—whatever that is. In a study of novices in the related practitioner field of medicine, the most stressful situation was the white water experience—having to make clinical decisions while very confused." (Skovholt, 2001, p. 56)

Celebrating Family Culture

In working with the Chen family, there are several considerations a therapist might keep in mind: the Chinese American culture, Danny as primary caretaker for Sean, and the implications of Leilani's head injury and how it may impact the family.

Jasmine, Leilani's mother, appears to have taken on much responsibility for her home, her husband, and Danny. "Women in Asian families believe that their family role is to monitor the emotional well being of their families" and are involved in the family's daily activities, solving problems and communicating events and issues to the father. It is not unusual for Asian women to feel closer to their children than to their husbands due to the more distant role of many Asian fathers in raising children (Ishii-Kuntz, 2000, p. 275).

Danny, although more identified with Western values, understood the significance of Jasmine's role in helping him with Sean. Respect for elders holds high significance in Asian families. Danny was unable to communicate verbally how he was feeling. Nonverbal communication is common in Asian families, and Danny was able to feel Jasmine's pressure and often noticed her tense facial gestures and robotlike behaviors when cleaning and caring for Sean, yet he could not let her know that he actually wanted her to leave the house and give him time alone. He did not want to risk disrespecting her good intentions.

Danny worried constantly about Leilani and feared that she would not survive and, if she did, would suffer residual effects of the head injury. The doctors told Danny that if she did survive she probably would experience memory loss and would have difficulty concentrating. Due to the unknown, Danny was not able to plan for Sean and how to provide care for him. Danny wondered if there was someone he could talk with about his situation and the pressure he was feeling.

Often, Chinese American clients perceive the need to obtain advice outside of the family as shameful. Initially, therapists should focus on concrete actions such as helping the client with forms or assisting with resources. Personal questions posed to the therapist and answered honestly help the client develop trust. The therapist might also keep communication rank in mind because addressing problems with authoritative figures such as the father is seen as inappropriate (Green, 2000, pp. 302–303).

- Describe how the Chens' traditional values and acculturation have impacted their lifestyle.

_____

_____

THERAPIST'S TOOLS

A critical aspect to successful therapeutic outcome is the therapeutic alliance. In working with the Chens, understanding the cultural and intergenerational issues is of paramount importance to establish rapport. Research suggests that the therapeutic alliance is associated with positive outcomes in therapy. Let's look at some ways you can ensure establishing a therapeutic alliance.

When therapists take an active role in the therapeutic process, clients experience a more positive outcome. Heightened activity of the therapist has a profound impact on the therapist and client relationship (Thomas, Werner-Wilson, & Murphy, 2005).

The active therapist, while guiding the client, always takes the client's cues, readiness, and participation into consideration. In working with Danny and his extended family, the therapist will need to gauge responses while evaluating the cultural differences between Asian families and the dominant culture; these differences could become a challenge when everybody is together in the same room.

TAKE A ONE-MINUTE VACATION

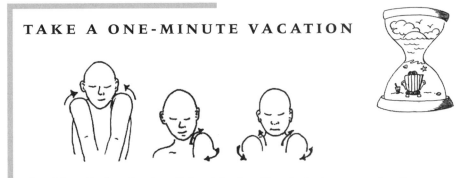

Shoulder Circles Slowly roll the right shoulder clockwise, squeezing it toward the ear, then down, forward, and up. Repeat several times. Reverse direction of circle and then repeat on the opposite side. Finally, rotate both shoulders at the same time; then repeat in opposite direction.

Exploratory Research and Resource Corner

- Where would you go to find out more information about head injury?

_____

_____

- How would you find out more about support for fathers of newborns?

  _____

  _____

- What other literature or resources would be helpful for you in working with the Chens?

  _____

  _____

Riding the Wave

Extended Family Session: Danny, Jasmine (mother-in-law), Meilei (Leilani's sister), and Therapist

Danny has been feeling ambivalent toward his extended family, particularly his mother-in-law Jasmine. On the one hand, he needs the guidance and support of Leilani's family, yet he feels intruded upon when they come to the house without calling and tell him how to feel and what to do. Danny asked his mother-in-law and oldest sister-in-law Meilei in law to join him with his therapist for a session. He hoped that he might respectfully express his feelings without creating an atmosphere of shame.

THERAPIST: (Greets Danny and extends hand out with a gentle bow to greet Jasmine and Meilei.)

DANNY: (Begins the session saying that he is scared and worried about Leilani.)

THERAPIST: It's only natural for you to have these feelings with Leilani in critical condition and caring for a newborn. (Turns to Jasmine.) It seems that you, Meilei, and others in the family have taken on a good deal of responsibility to help Danny and Leilani. It's wonderful that Danny has so much support, yet I'm thinking that visiting the hospital and helping Danny with Sean can be exhausting.

JASMINE: This is my duty. My mother is eighty-five years old and lives with us. She worked hard all of her life for the family and encourages me to stay strong for the family as she has been. My husband George works long hours and he worries about Leilani; I try to ease his worry and take care of him when he comes home at night. We are all concerned about Leilani and are doing our best to help.

MEILEI: Grandma is amazing; she still cooks every night for all of us, and not microwave style, fresh foods from scratch. (She smiles with warmth.) Leilani always has so much energy and spunk; it's devastating to see her just lying there.

JASMINE: (Has tears in her eyes.)

THERAPIST: I know how difficult it is for everyone, yet everyone has their own needs and ways to deal with Leilaini's accident and the joy of Sean's birth at the same time.

DANNY: (Looks around at everyone, feels he can't tell them to back off, can feel anxiety rising.) Yes, grandma is amazing, all of you are amazing; I appreciate all of your help, and grandma's great dinners.

THERAPIST: (Turns to Danny.) I hear how grateful you are for the help. I wonder, Danny, with all of the help you are getting is there anything else you might need at this time? Take a moment to reflect, close your eyes, take your time, and listen to your instincts. See what awareness you have.

DANNY: (Sits for a minute or two, eyes closed. He looks up and speaks quietly, softly, without anxiety.) Sometimes I'm so overwhelmed I don't even know my own feelings and thoughts. I very much need to have some time alone with myself and with Sean. We need each other right now.

THERAPIST: Alone time can be very healing. I wonder how Jasmine and Meilei can support you in this way.

DANNY: (Looks up toward Jasmine.) Would it be okay if you called me before coming over?

JASMINE: Yes, I hear you. I can be there when you need me. I don't mean to intrude; I only want to help.

DANNY: Thank you, Jasmine. Sometimes I need to think about Leilani before the accident to remember the good times.

JASMINE: I understand, I also need time to be alone and I use my meditations for this. It also helps to make me more aware. I have a new meditation pillow that I would like to give you.

DANNY: This would be wonderful; it feels like ages since I've had a good meditation. I appreciate this offering. You have been so generous with your time, I forget that you are suffering too; I would like to make dinner for the family and give grandma a break. (Everyone laughs.)

JASMINE AND MEILEI: That would be great!

THERAPIST: Thank you for coming today. (Slightly bows head and speaks to Jasmine and Meilei.) It was an honor to meet you.

- What are your thoughts about Jasmine?

_____

_____

- Describe your perceptions of how the therapist handled the session.

_____

_____

- How might Danny be feeling at this time?

_____

_____

- What strengths are you aware of in the family?

_____

_____

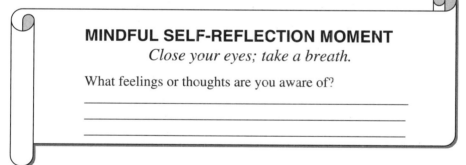

MINDFUL SELF-REFLECTION MOMENT
Close your eyes; take a breath.

What feelings or thoughts are you aware of?

_____

_____

_____

Beyond Treatment

Danny continued with his therapist, spent more time with Sean, and began a program of daily meditation. On several occasions he joined Leilani's family at the Buddhist temple for services, which helped him to feel more grounded. This was also another way to spend time with Sean and the family without feeling overwhelmed by visits at the house.

When Leilani came home she joined Danny in therapy after a few months. She was dealing with short-term memory loss, migraines, and difficulty concentrating, which frustrated her and caused her to feel inadequate.

She needed time to reconnect with Sean, Danny, and herself. Danny organized a family gathering with his family and Leilani's to celebrate Sean's birth and to welcome Leilani home. Leilani's family was excited to help with the cooking and preparations.

- Where would you go from here with the Chens?

_____

_____

REFERENCES

Green, J. W. (2000). (Ed.), _Cultural awareness in the human services: A multi-ethnic approach_ (pp. 287–319). Needham Heights, MA: Allyn & Bacon.

Kim-Ju, G. M., Liem, R. (2003) ethnic self awareness as a function of ethnic group status, group composition, and ethnic identity orientation. _Cultural Diversity and Ethnic Minority Psychology, 9_(3) 289–302

Skovholt, T. M. (2001). _The resilient practitioner: Burnout preventions and self-care strategies for counselors, therapists, teachers, and health professionals._ Needham Heights, MA: Allyn & Bacon p. 56.

Thomas, S. E. G., Werner-Wilson, R. J., & Murphy, M. J. (2005). Influence of therapist and client behaviors on therapy alliance. _Contemporary Family Therapy, 27_(1), 19–35.

Yu-Wen, Ying; Coombs, M., Lee, P. A. (1999) Family intergenerational relationship of Asian American Adolescents, _Cultural Diversity and Ethnic Minority Psychology 5_(4) 350–363

SUGGESTED READING

Buki, L. P., Ma, T. C., Strom, R. D., & Strom, S. K. (2003). Chinese immigrant mothers of adolescents: Self-perceptions of acculturation effects on parenting. _Cultural Diversity and Ethnic Minority Psychology, 9_(2), 127–140.

Buki, L. P., Tsung-Chieh, Ma, Strom, R.D., Strom, S.K. (2003) Chinese immigrant mothers of adolescents: self-perceptions of acculturation effects on parenting. _Cultural diversity and Ethnic Minority Psychology 9_(2) 127–140.

Falsafi, N. (2001). The use of holistic concepts in professional practice. _Journal of Holistic Nursing, 19_(4), 390–392.

Fang, S. R. S., & Wark, L. (1998). Developing cross-cultural competence with traditional Chinese Americans in family therapy: Background information and the initial therapeutic contact. _Contemporary Family Therapy, 20_(10), 59–77.

Gordon, J. S. (2004). The White House Commission on Complementary and Alternative Medicine Policy and the Future of Healthcare. _Alternative Therapies in Health and Medicine, 10_(5), 20–23.

Hong, G. K., & Domokos-Cheng Ham, M. (2001). _Psychotherapy and counseling with Asian American clients: A practical guide._ Thousand Oaks, CA; Sage.

Ishii-Kuntz, M. (2000). Diversity within Asian American Families. In D. H. Demo, K. R. Allen, & M. A. Fine (Eds.), _Handbook of family diversity_ (pp. 274–292). New York: Oxford University Press.

Iwamasa, G. Y. (2002). Relationships among Asian American Women. *Cultural Diversity and Ethnic Minority Psychology, 8*(1), 60–62.

Jensen, O. K., & Thulstrup, A. M. (2001). Gender differences of post-traumatic headache and other post-commotos symptoms. A follow-up study after a period of 9–12 months. *Ugeskrift for laeger* (Denmark), *163*(37), 5029–5033.

Kreitzer, M. J., & Disch, J. (2003). Leading the way: The Gillette nursing summit on integrated health and healing. *Alternative Therapies, 9*(1), 3A–10A.

LaRossa, R. (2000). Fatherhood and social change. In M. B. Zinn, P. Hondagneu-Sotello, & M. A. Messner (Eds.), *Gender through the prism of difference* (pp. 298–309). Needham Heights, MA: Allyn & Bacon.

Lawson, D. M., & Brossart, D. F. (2003). Intergenerational transmission: Individuation and intimacy across three generations. *Family Process Winter, 40*(4), 429–443.

Leung, P., & Cheung, M. (2001). Competencies in practice evaluations with Asian American individuals and families. In R. Fong & S. Furuto (Eds.), *Culturally competent practice, skills, interventions, and evaluations* (pp. 426–437). Needham Heights, MA: Allyn & Bacon.

Louie, M. L. (2003). Gender bias in the Chinese American family: Its effects on Chinese American women's self-concept. (Doctoral dissertation). *Dissertation Abstracts International, A: The Humanities and Social Sciences, 63*(1), 375A. (UMI No DA3040101)

Mayou, R. A., Black, J., & Bryant, B. (2000). Unconsciousness, amnesia and psychiatric symptoms following road traffic accident injury. *The British Journal of Psychiatry: The Journal of Mental Science, 177,* 540–545.

Ponsford, J., Willmott, C., Rothwell, A., Cameron, P., Kelly, A. M., Nelms, R., Curran, C., & Ng, K. (2000). Factors influencing outcome following mild traumatic brain injury in adults. *Journal of the International Neuropsychological Society, 6*(5), 568–579.

Quinn, C., Chandler, C., & Moraska, A. (2002). Massage therapy and frequency of chronic tension headaches. *American Journal of Public Health, 92*(10), 1657–1661.

Rodegast, P., & Stanton, J. (1989). *Emmanuel's Book II: The choice for love,* New York: Bantam Books.

Stocker, R., Burgi, U., Keller, E., & Imhof, H. (2000). Clinical management of acute head injury. *Schweizerische medizinische Wochenschrift* (Switzerland), *130*(42), 1544–1556.

Yip, T., & Cross, W. E., Jr. (2004). A daily diary study of mental health and community involvement outcomes for three Chinese American social identities. *Cultural Diversity and Ethnic Minority Psychology, 10*(4), 394–408.

8 The Community Heals a Family: The Story of the LaSotos

If you've become a stodgy old crank, ask a child to teach you to play. When feeling uptight, worried, or in a stew, pause for a silly moment; think silly, act silly, walk silly, talk silly. If you're hopelessly out of practice, look to your child for a cue, you won't find a more willing coach. Your child's laughter is the best remedy for what ails you.

Ford, 1995, p. 93

Getting Started

"Will somebody please help us? Our baby is covered with blisters, we don't know what to do," Pilar cried out to the family therapist, who was meeting with the LaSotos for the first time.

What feeling and thoughts are you aware of right now?

_____

_____

Pilar and Acacio, a young Portuguese American couple, came to the Ocean Family Service Center seeking help for their six-month-old daughter Brittany. They entered the session feeling upset and frustrated with the social service department, and they reported that their daughter was suffering from a genetic skin condition that caused her to blister upon physical contact. They needed supplies to wrap her after treating the blisters, and special diapers that would not irritate her skin. Pilar and Acacio wanted to help their daughter, yet they found themselves bickering daily about their situation, which caused additional stress on their relationship. Acacio had difficulty accepting Brittany's disease and complained that Pilar did not pay attention to him anymore.

Session with Pilar, Acacio, and Therapist

THERAPIST: I'm pleased to meet you, and I am interested to hear about your concerns regarding Brittany.

PILAR: Our baby is suffering and Acacio just runs away and leaves the house. I have to deal with popping her blisters and everything else alone. I'm so scared.

ACACIO: She's exaggerating. I love Brittany and am here for them both. Sometimes I just need space to get away. I feel so much, I don't know what to do.

THERAPIST: I'm hearing from both of you that you are feeling overwhelmed and frightened with Brittany's illness and both of you have different ways of dealing with your feelings.

PILAR: I want to feel some peace at home with Acacio. It's so stressful caring for Brittany. My feelings are so deep sometimes I don't know where to turn for relief.

ACACIO: It tears me apart to see our daughter suffering every day. Those needles inflict more pain and I just can't do it! I just can't hurt our baby.

THERAPIST: I'm hearing your concerns and realize that both of you need to talk about what's happening to you as well as what's going on with Brittany. I also realize how difficult it is for you to get out of the house. Let's talk about ways to help you both. First, I'd like to offer you the opportunity to have our sessions at your home to make it more convenient for us to meet.

PILAR: That's a relief; I was trying to imagine how we could get here, particularly when the winter comes. I appreciate your flexibility.

ACACIO: Thank you; I realize that just talking today helped me put some things into perspective.

THERAPIST: It's settled; let's set up our next appointment.

• Describe your impressions of Pilar and Acacio.

_____

_____

• Put yourself in Brittany's tragic situation. What might she be experiencing?

_____

_____

• What interventions might you consider?

_____

_____

THOUGHTS TO PONDER

The literature on children with disabilities notes that fathers and mothers respond differently to their child:

Mothers	Fathers
More open with emotions	Less emotional
More concerned with the burden of the daily care of the child	Focus on long-term problems (i.e., financial)
	Fathers who are less involved with the daily interactions with the child have long periods of denial about the disability and its implications (Naseef, 2001, p. 126)

A Window into the Past

Pilar and Acacio

Pilar is an outgoing, gregarious, twenty-five-year-old Portuguese American woman who can muster a smile in the most difficult situations. She has many friends, and people seek out her companionship. She is forthright and speaks her mind, letting people know where she stands on issues. Acacio is a more reserved, quiet, twenty-five-year-old Portuguese American man who has an interest in science, cars, and the environment. He also likes to build things and is usually involved in a project at home. He has few friends and spends most of his time with Pilar and family.

Acacio works as a fisherman in the tradition of the LaSoto men in a small village in Massachusetts, a community inhabited by Portuguese whalers for many generations. He enjoys his work, loves nature, and loves exploring the environment. Pilar works at a local hair salon. She has worked there for the past eight years.

Pilar and Acacio dreamed of having a family. They both were born into large Portuguese families. After dating for one year, Pilar and Acacio decided to marry. Within the first year Brittany was born. Pilar worked with a midwife, a friend of the family, and enjoyed the attention and simple guidance provided for her throughout the pregnancy from aunts and cousins. Acacio was busy making room in their small apartment for the new arrival.

Extended Family

Both Pilar and Acacio enjoy the benefits and challenges of a large family. Acacio has two brothers and a sister, and Pilar has two sisters and a brother. Both Pilar and Acacio are close to their siblings, and over the years, all of the siblings have become friendly and enjoy socializing on holidays and family occasions. Acacio spends time after work in the local tavern with his male relatives and friends, a tradition after a day of fishing. This is a time for the men to share stories openly without their wives present. Pilar spends time visiting with the women in the extended family. The women do not socialize in the taverns, and only on special occasions are they allowed to go to taverns with their husbands. The women often feel the isolation of maintaining their traditional role in the family yet want to experience more independence. This is often the topic of conversation when the women meet, yet they do not pursue their desire for more autonomy. Women who want to spend time away from the home without their husbands are frowned upon and viewed as engaging in suspicious behavior.

Acacio complains that his parents are demanding and judgmental; consequently, he seeks constant attention from Pilar. Acacio's parents live nearby, and they hold resentment toward Acacio. They had a girl chosen for Acacio, a friend of the family, and were disappointed that he chose Pilar instead. Pilar is very close to her mother, Florinda, who was very involved in Pilar's pregnancy, offered advice, and spent evenings helping to plan for the new arrival. Jose, Pilar's father, works long hours and is only superficially involved in the family's day-to-day events. Nonetheless, Pilar and Acacio are expected to listen to Jose's advice even though Pilar is an adult with her own family.

- How might Pilar's cultural traditions impact her life today?

  _____

  _____

- How might the change in Acacio's life today impact his interests and prior lifestyle?

  _____

  _____

- What are your thoughts about the socialization of Portuguese men and women?

  _____

  _____

Embracing the Essence

Pilar tells the therapist that "Brittany was the most beautiful baby I'd ever seen. She had a pink round face, a button nose, heart-shaped lips, and beautiful golden hair formed in small ringlets. I cried with joy when I first saw our tiny bundle. Two days after we brought Brittany home from the hospital, we noticed that she was turning yellow. The jaundice did not seem to be a problem, yet three days later small blisters began appearing on her body. No one at the hospital seemed to know what was causing the blisters, and Brittany spent the first days of her birth as an experiment, with tubes, needles in her head, bandages, and a host of physicians trying to figure out what was happening to our baby. Brittany was born a beauty and soon looked like a monster. I cried relentlessly, searching for answers, feeling powerless."

The Traumatic Fate

Brittany was brought to a special children's hospital and diagnosed with a rare skin condition called epidermolysis bullosa (EB), also known as the blistering disease. Epidermolysis is a group of blistering skin conditions. The skin is so fragile in people with EB that even minor rubbing may cause blistering. At times, the person with EB may not be aware of rubbing or injuring the skin, yet blisters will develop. Brittany was diagnosed with the simplex form of EB.

Dowling Meara epidermolysis bullosa simplex is a generalized form of EBS and usually begins with blistering that is evident at birth or shortly afterward. In a localized, mild form called Weber-Cockayne, blisters rarely extend beyond the feet and hands. In some subtypes of EBS, the blisters occur over widespread areas of the body. Other signs may include thickened skin on the palms of the hands and soles of the feet; rough, thickened, or absent fingernails or toenails; and blistering of the soft tissues inside the mouth. In EBS, the faulty genes are those that provide instructions for producing keratin, a fibrous protein in the top layer of skin. As a result, the skin splits in the epidermis, producing a blister.

Pilar and Acacio were confused, frightened, and filled with despair when they were told that this disease was incurable. Pilar was fighting for her child's life and trying to hold onto her senses so she could gather information. Acacio was unable to face the fate of his newborn child. His dream was shattered, and he dealt with his feelings by running away. Acacio cried to his brothers and male relatives about his feelings regarding Brittany, yet he could not share his feelings with Pilar. As a Portuguese man, he felt he needed to be strong and take care of the finances and work on the house. He often stayed out late and became argumentative with Pilar. Pilar was working day and night to care for Brittany, who endured endless suffering. In addition to the time spent caring for Brittany, Pilar and Acacio could not afford the supplies needed to care for her properly.

Care of the Newborn with Epidermolysis Bullosa

To protect the skin of the newborn afflicted with epidermolysis bullosa it is critical that precautions be taken to prevent the incidence of blistering. In addition, special care must be taken to delicately treat the existing blisters to prevent infection.

Prevention of Blisters

Handle gently. Avoid lifting babies or children from under the arms; instead, place one hand beneath the bottom and another beneath the head/neck to lift. A pillow, egg-crate (foam) pad, or sheepskin may be used beneath the baby to prevent friction against the skin while lifting and holding.

Do not rub skin. Since blisters can be caused by friction, the skin should be patted rather than rubbed. Before blood tests or immunizations, the area can be cleansed by gently pressing or patting the alcohol pad against the skin.

Dress the baby in loose-fitting clothes. Clothing that rubs the skin may cause blisters. Avoid or alter clothing that features binding elastic. Avoid harsh buttons, snaps, and zippers. Nonbinding diapers or cloth diapers may be used.

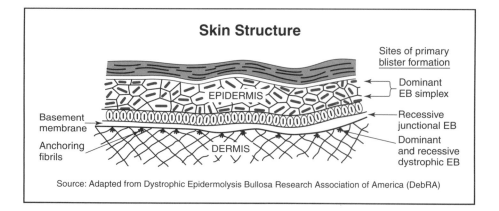

Source: Adapted from Dystrophic Epidermolysis Bullosa Research Association of America (DebRA)

Avoid excessive heat: Overheating tends to increase skin fragility. Maintain a moderate environmental temperature (including your car) and do not overdress the baby.

Do not use adhesives on the skin. Tape or adhesive bandages should not be applied to the skin because they may cause blistering.

Lubricate the skin. Aquaphor or Vaseline will help decrease friction.

Pad bony prominences. Gauze sponges, secured by rolled gauze, may be used to pad elbows, heels, and knees if infant gets blisters from kicking against the sheet in the crib. Soft socks may be placed over lubricated hands and feet to prevent blisters.

Blister Care and Prevention of Infection
Wash hands before administering skin care. Hand washing is the most effective measure to control infection.

Do not remove clothing or dressings that are stuck to the skin. Materials that are stuck to the skin should be soaked until they can be removed easily. This can be done at bath time (in the tub) or by applying room-temperature water or a soaked compress directly to the bandage.

Cleanse skin daily. Skin may be cleaned with a very mild soap.

Drain blisters. Blisters tend to increase in size if they are allowed to remain intact. For this reason, most blisters should be drained when they are about the size of a dime. Sterile needles or lancets may be used to puncture the side of the blister roof. The blister roof should be left intact to facilitate healing and comfort.

Apply topical antibiotics to lesions. Mild, over-the-counter antibiotics are effective in preventing infection and may be rotated every month or two to discourage bacterial resistance.

Apply nonadherent dressings. After application of topical antibiotics, a non-stick dressing should be applied to denuded or unprotected areas. Next, rolled gauze is wrapped around the nonadherent dressing and is then secured with a tubular dressing retainer. The dressing retainer will prevent tape tearing the skin.

Change dressing daily. Daily dressing changes are recommended and can be coordinated with a bath or cleansing of the skin.

Source: Adapted from http://www.debra.org/modules.php?op=modload&name=News&file =article&sid=15#11

- What are some of the issues Pilar and Acacio might face in having a child with a hereditary gene deficiency?

  _____

  _____

- What clinical intervention would support the LaSotos at this time?

  _____

  _____

- What strengths do you see in both Acacio and Pilar?

  _____

  _____

MINDFUL SELF-REFLECTION MOMENT
Close your eyes; take a breath.

What feelings or thoughts are you aware of?

_____

_____

_____

Exploratory Research and Resource Corner

- What steps might you take to find out more information to help the LaSotos?

  _____

  _____

- What professionals or services would assist you in treating the LaSotos?

  _____

  _____

- Describe some activities that might help Pilar and Acacio feel more empowered and connected to each other.

  _____

  _____

Celebrating Family Culture

Between 1899 and 1910, more than 8 million illegal aliens over the age of fourteen immigrated to the United States. Of all those groups, the Portuguese had the highest illiteracy rate, at 68 percent. The new immigrants relied on relatives or debts to Portugal to help finance their move to the United States, and most did not have money to make the trip on their own. "The Portuguese arriving in the United States at the turn of the nineteenth century were a culturally homogeneous group. The same rural and island roots, the same religious beliefs, the same literacy rates and the same overwhelming lack of skills and financial resources characterized the members of this migrant group" (Ioannis and Baganha, 1991, p. 280).

Many Portuguese emigrated to the United States between 1860 and 1930, and most settled in Massachusetts, California, and Hawaii. The Portuguese who settled in Massachusetts were often crew members for whaling and merchant fleets in the nineteenth century. As early as 1860, the Portuguese were employed in whaling, fishing, and agriculture. The men maintained the status as "head of household." The LaSotos maintained their trade of fishing and whaling for generations in the small fishing town in which they lived.

Acacio was fortunate to have inherited a small parcel of land, on which he built a small home for his family. When his great grandparents emigrated to the United States, several large families purchased land that would be unaffordable today. The small whaling town has now become a popular resort for city summer vacationers.

Both Pilar and Acacio were born into families of whalers. As with many immigrants, their great grandparents sought economic opportunity in the United States. Both Acacio and Pilar maintained their Portuguese traditions but did not plan to have large families, as their parents and grandparents did.

Pilar and Acacio live in a low-income rural fishing village and have suffered the hardships of seasonal work. The families have worked together to farm their land and sell produce to supplement their incomes. Without social, family, and community support it would be difficult for them to survive. Acacio has been blessed with the talent of carpentry as well as being a successful fisherman. He made all of the furniture in the house with the help of his brothers and cousins and artistically crafted a large changing table for Brittany, with cubbies for all of the supplies needed for treating the blisters.

Pilar and Acacio want to be able to care for their child and often feel ashamed to ask for help from local government agencies. For generations the extended families and friends have been able to support each other in time of need. The LaSotos have faced the challenges of living in a rural community with limited resources, earning a low income due to seasonal work, and parenting a physically challenged child.

- How has the LaSotos' culture influenced their lives?

  _____

  _____

- What are the strengths inherent in the culture of the LaSotos?

  _____

  _____

- How might the extended family impair or help the LaSotos in raising Brittany?

  _____

  _____

THERAPISTS' TOOLS

In working with the LaSotos, the therapist will experience many emotions that can easily take one out of the moment and affect the ability to be congruent. Satir advises that therapists become congruent at all times during the family session. She notes that "when therapists are congruent, they are fully present, whole, centered, and in a state of peaceful harmony" (Lum, 2002, p. 182). Satir identifies four factors that are important for the therapist's development of self.

1. *Increase self-esteem.* When therapists feel good about themselves, they are better able to trust their instincts, feel more confident in their clinical skills, and are better able to accept who they are. When therapists accept their own strengths and maintain self-care, they increase self-esteem.
2. *Foster better choice making.* Satir believes that there are three choices for any decision, and therapists must not get stuck in an either–or situation but must make room for further exploration and other choices.
3. *Increase responsibility.* Therapists are encouraged to work through their own unresolved issues and to respond to their clients with compassion without judgment. To truly hear what is behind the words and interaction of clients will take therapeutic artistry on the part of the therapist. Therapists will be more effective if they have the ability to respond to both the context and the process of therapy, and this involves integrating an awareness of personal ethics with the skills of a therapeutic technician.
4. *Develop congruence.* Therapists develop congruence by maintaining harmony with themselves, others, and the environment. Finding the balance of what we feel inside and how we perceive the world outside is the goal (Lum, 2002).

- What are some of your personal challenges in maintaining congruence?

Riding the Wave

Pilar tells the therapist, "I contacted our local social services department and asked for help with Brittany. I cleaned her up and they made an appointment to visit our home. When they came to our home, the worker commented how clean it was and how well cared for Brittany looked. Two weeks later we received a letter stating that the worker denied services for our baby. Acacio became enraged, threw food and garbage around the house, and dressed Brittany in raggy clothes. He was yelling like a wild man. Following this tirade we called our local social services agency and a new worker came to our home and decided that we needed assistance. We had to look as if we were crazy and negligent before anyone listened." Pilar and Acacio were offered installation of bathroom equipment for people with disabilities and some assistance in purchasing supplies. The bathroom is equipped with a wider door and room and wider tub with rails. It was not nearly enough. Pilar's family offered some money and supplies; Acacio's parents continued their distance. Brittany needed to be changed every fifteen minutes; the gauze, medications, needles, and clothes were draining their paychecks.

- What treatment techniques would you implement to support the LaSotos?

_____

_____

- Would you intervene with the social service agency? If so, in what way?

_____

_____

- Would you engage the extended family? If so, how?

_____

_____

TAKE A ONE-MINUTE VACATION
Three-Part Breath

Think about how water fills up a glass. It first goes into the bottom and fills up to the top; when emptied it first empties from the top and then the bottom. Imagine that your lungs are like the glass.

1. Get comfortable; sit with your back straight and chest lifted or lie down on your back. Slowly breathe in through your nose,
2. Notice how the breath moves from your lungs and lifts from your tummy, ribs, chest, and shoulders. Notice your belly filling up like a balloon.
3. When you exhale, let the breath ooze out of your lungs slowly, like a balloon losing its air until it is empty.

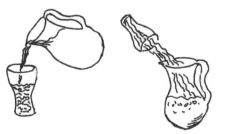

First meeting, with Acacio
and a Town Council member

ACACIO: Thank you for seeing me today. Any help is appreciated.

COUNCIL MEMBER: We are concerned about Brittany and know how difficult it must be for you and Pilar.

ACACIO: You can't even imagine how difficult it is. Can you help supply cotton diapers for Brittany? They are the only diapers that minimize friction to her skin.

COUNCIL MEMBER: I believe we can help you with the diapers.

ACACIO: Our family is most grateful for any assistance and help you can give us.

(The council sent a case of diapers, which last three weeks.)

Second meeting, with Acacio
and the Town Council President

ACACIO: Pilar and I want to thank you for the diapers. They were a great help; unfortunately, they are gone.

PRESIDENT OF COUNCIL: All of them!?

ACACIO: Yes; Brittany often has to be changed every fifteen minutes. If any urine or feces touches the blisters, it burns and can cause infection.

PRESIDENT OF COUNCIL: I'll see what I can do.

ACACIO: We very much appreciate your help. Would you like to meet Brittany?

PRESIDENT OF COUNCIL: Oh yes; please, do bring her in.

Third meeting, with Acacio, Brittany,
and the Town Council President

Acacio brings Brittany in for a visit. The President exclaims with warmth that the community has adopted Brittany as its "community child," and two weeks later ten cases of diapers arrive at Pilar and Acacio's house; this supply lasts nine months.

THOUGHTS TO PONDER

Examples of Creative Health Partnerships—Primary Care and Prevention

1. Involve community members in the design and delivery of services.
2. Identify people at risk for health problems during crisis events.
3. Outreach to people by providing coordinated health success in accessible community sites or in homes of families.
4. Emphasize community ownership of health problems and solutions.
5. Cut across traditional professional boundaries to provide holistic and coordinated care.
6. Create new structures to integrate traditionally fragmented systems of care.

(Adapted from Poole & Van Hook, 1998 p. 3)

MINDFUL SELF-REFLECTION MOMENT
Close your eyes; take a breath.

What feelings or thoughts are you aware of?

_____
_____
_____

Beyond Treatment

The town council continued to support the family by giving food, baby necessities, and holiday and birthday gifts. There was a ray of hope when Pilar heard of a scientist who had a cure for EB. The community council called Pilar and Acacio stating that they had a surprise Christmas present for them. When Pilar and Acacio arrived at the council office, they were given a check for $10,000 for the treatment. Part of the money was raised by local stores, which placed empty fishbowls at checkout counters so customers could make donations to help raise money for the treatment. Brittany was officially called the "community baby." Unfortunately, her treatment was excruciatingly painful and unsuccessful. Nevertheless, the LaSotos did not give up hope.

A local shoemaker crafted special shoes for Brittany that had soft sheepskin cushioning. One of Pilar's friends learned how to pop Brittany's blisters to give Pilar relief from the daily routine. Friends and family rotated to assist Pilar and Acacio with household chores, cooking, and shopping. Pilar and Acacio never left Brittany with anyone, but they welcomed the visits for companionship and assistance.

- What are your thoughts about the role of community?

  _____

  _____

- What challenges might Pilar and Acacio face if they decide to have more children?

  _____

  _____

- Where would you go from here with treatment?

  _____

  _____

THOUGHTS TO PONDER

"The sort of health that Nature has planned for us behaves very much like weather conditions: there is no such thing as a permanent high-pressure area without the storms from encroaching frontal systems. There is no such thing as continuous health without the risk of death. In this regard, it seems, we are in no way wise independent of Nature; rather we live as an integral part of the elemental landscape of our origin" (Ziegler, 1991, p. 96).

REFERENCES

Ioannis, M., & Baganha, B. (1991). The social mobility of Portuguese immigrants in the United States at the turn of the nineteenth century. *International Migration Review, 25,* (94), 277–302.

Kilpatrick, A. C. & Holland, T. P. (2003) *Working with Families an Integrative Model by Level of Need.* Allyn and Bacon Boston chap 13 Family in the community 218–229.

Lum, W. (2002). The use of self of the therapist. *Contemporary Family Therapy, 24*(1), 181–197.

Naseef, R. A. (2001). *Special children, challenged parents: The struggles and rewards of raising a child with a disability.* Baltimore, MD: Paul H. Brookes.

Ziegler, A. J. (1991). *Meeting the shadow: The hidden power of the dark side of human nature,* p.92.

SUGGESTED READING

Aboim, S. (2003). The development of domestic structures. *Sociologia Problemas e Practices, 43,* 13–30.

Dossey, L. (1991) The light of health, the shadow of illness in Ziegler, A. J. *Meeting the Shadow: The Hidden Power of the Dark Side of Human Nature,* Penguin/Putnam, NY p. 91–93

Ford, J. (1995). *Wonderful ways to love a child.* Emeryville, CA: Conari Press.

Henderson, L. (2000). The knowledge and use of alternative therapeutic techniques by social work practitioners: A descriptive study. *Social Work Health Care, 30*(3), 55–71.

Lavery, S. H., Smith, M. L., Esparza, A. A., Hrushow, A., Moore, M. & Reed, D. F. (2005).

McIntyre, T. M., & Augusto, F. (1999). The martyr adaptation syndrome: Spuchological sequelae in the adaptation of Portuguese-speaking immigrant women. *Cultural Diversity and Ethnic Minority Psychology, 5*(4), 387–402.

Napoli, M., & Santin-Gonzalez, E. (2001). Intensive home-based treatment and wellness services for American Indian families. *Families and Society, 82,* 315–324.

O'Donnell, J., & Giovannoni, J. M. (2000). Consumer perceptions of outreach and marketing strategies for family resource centers. *Journal of Community Practice, 8*(2), 71–89.

Pina, A. (2003). Intellectual spaces of practice and hope: power and culture in Portugal from the 1940's to the present. *Cultural Studies, 17*(6), 751–766.

Poole, F. L., & Van Hook, M. (1998). Retooling for community health partnerships in primary care and prevention. *Health & Social Work, 22*(1), 2–4.

Shannon, P. (2004). Barriers to family-centered services for infants and toddlers with developmental delays. *Social Work Journal, 49*(2), 301–308.

Sinclair, S. L., & Taylor, B. A. (2004). Unpacking the tough guise: Toward a discursive approach for working with men in family therapy. *Contemporary Family Therapy, 26*(4), 389–408.

Hennessey Lavery S., Smith, M. L., Esparza, A. A., Hrushow, A., Moore, M., and Reed, O. F. (2005) The Community Action Model: A community-driven model designed to address disparities in health. *American Journal of Public Health, 95*(4), 611–616.

The Dystrophic Epidermolysis Bullosa Research Association of America Inc. (DebRA), 5 West 36th Street, Suite 404, New York, NY 10018, phone 212-868-1573, e-mail staff@debra.org

The National EB Registry, Jo-David Fine, M.D., M.P.H., c/o Dermatology Associates of Kentucky, 250 Fountain Court, Lexington, KY 40509, phone 859-363-4444, e-mail ebregistry@daklex.com.

Vandergriff-Avery, A. M. (2002). Rural families speak: A qualitative investigation of stress protective and crisis recovery strategies utilized by rural low-income women and their families. *Dissertation Abstracts International, A: The Humanities and Social Sciences, 62*(12), 4350A–4351A.

William, Jr. (1982) *And yet they come: Portuguese immigration from the Azores to the United States.* Center for Migration studies, 209 Flagg Place, Staten Island, NY 10304.

9 A Tiny Toddler Loses Her Taste: The Story of the Russos

*Parenting is a two way street. As you take them by the hand,
they will take you by the heart.*
Ford, 1995, p. 7

Getting Started

LORETTA: It's been two weeks and my eighteen-month-old Ariel has not eaten a morsel of food. Everything else seems normal; she just does not eat. Can she survive without food?

VINNY: We need to take that bottle away and then she will eat; even my family agrees.

THERAPIST: I'd like to hear your story. Let's start from the beginning.

What reactions are you aware of right now?

_____

_____

Loretta and Vinny tell their story about their daughter Ariel, who is eighteen months old. Loretta was getting ready to take Ariel's bottle away during the month of March, when Ariel stopped eating. It is now May, and Ariel will only take a bottle. Ariel is having difficulty sleeping and will not allow Loretta to leave the room without her. Loretta says, "We are joined at the hip. She feels like a monkey, holding on for dear life."

Loretta is feeling overwhelmed since family members are offering different suggestions about how to deal with this difficult situation. Advice from Vinny's family included the following: Take the bottle away, which might force Ariel to eat. Don't let her leave the table until she eats. Don't offer her any food until she gets an appetite. All of these suggestions have brought the Russos into a tailspin.

- Discuss what would be your first step in working with Loretta and Vinny.

_____

_____

- Describe what you think may be going on with Ariel.

_____

_____

- What do you know about childhood eating disorders?

_____

_____

THOUGHTS TO PONDER

Research has found that eating disorders in young children are an important prediction of suffering in children and adolescence. Parents play a significant role in children's self-perceptions by their behavior toward the child (Edmunds & Hill, 1999; Mariachi & Cohen, 1990).

A Window into the Past

Loretta

Loretta is the youngest of five children—three sisters and two brothers—born to a large southern Italian family. Her nickname in the family was "tiny" because she was very small and petite, much like Ariel. She describes herself as extremely shy and states that she depended upon Rose, her older sister by fifteen months, who was outgoing and verbal, to speak for her. Her fear of rejection and timid demeanor carried through adulthood. Loretta often criticized herself about her timid way and hoped to become more assertive. She liked to please others and often sought approval for her gourmet talents from family members and friends.

Vinny

Vinny is the youngest of four children born to a large northern Italian family. Like Loretta, his role in the family was the "pleaser." He often helped friends and family fix their houses and helped with other projects. Like Loretta, his older brother (by eighteen months) Anthony was more outgoing and verbal and had a knack for business. Vinny enjoyed playing the guitar and works as an architect. Vinny is opinionated and likes to be seen as knowledgeable. He regrettably finds himself criticizing Loretta, then feels remorseful, yet he has difficulty changing this behavior. He says he loves Loretta and she will always be his sweetheart. He likes that she is an "old-fashioned girl."

Loretta and Vinny

Loretta and Vinny dated for eighteen months before getting engaged, and they married after two years of courtship. They bought a small house and have three children, Chelsea, eight years old, Joanna, six years old, and Ariel, eighteen months. Loretta quit her job before Chelsea was born and has been a homemaker since then. She spends most of her time cleaning and organizing the house, often redecorating, yet she feels something is missing in her life. Vinny complains that Loretta is obsessed with her need for order and cleanliness. Vinny is a fussy eater and does not like to try new foods, which is a constant disappointment to Loretta, who is proud and confident of her gourmet talents. Loretta harbors an underlying anger due to her difficulty to express herself. She worked in accounts for a bank before marrying Vinny, yet she would have liked to become a chef. She does not like to depend upon Vinny for money, particularly since they often don't agree about finances, which intensifies her feelings of dependency. When Ariel was born, Loretta had to postpone returning to work. She was looking forward to being with adults in the workplace. Loretta and Vinny have felt frustrated with the older girls, who have had difficulty expressing themselves. The girls are shy and don't speak in front of strangers and keep to themselves. Ariel shows affection toward her sisters, initiates play with them, and imitates them during play. Vinny sometimes feels rejected by Loretta and misses having intimate time with her. She is tired at the end of the day and goes to sleep early. Vinny yearns to be closer to Loretta.

- What clinical interventions might strengthen Loretta and Vinny's relationship?

  _____

  _____

- What avenues of treatment would you explore?

  _____

  _____

- What are the family's strengths?

  _____

  _____

- What are your thoughts about Chelsea and Joanna's shy behavior?

  _____

  _____

THOUGHTS TO PONDER

"Although their cognitive understanding is limited, children three and younger nonetheless feel and react to the death of an important person in their lives with strong emotions and confusion. Children's history and memory will affect the dimensions of their grief; the more frequent and positive the contact, the more acutely very young children will be aware of person's absence. A grandfather who lived down the street and was seen daily by a toddler will be missed much more that the great aunt who visited only for holiday dinners" (Norris-Shortle, Young and Williams, 1993, p. 737).

Embracing the Essence

Vinny's father died after a long battle with cancer in March, three days before Ariel stopped eating. One month prior to Vinny's father's death, Vinny spent many days and nights visiting with his father at his parents' home. He often cried when he came home and frequently slept at his parents' house, which disrupted the family routine. Sometimes Ariel went with Vinny to visit "Poppy," who eventually died in Ariel's presence. The family was gathered in the bedroom while Vinny's father took his last breath. Ariel was in the room. Loretta was shopping with Chelsea and Joanna, and Vinny took Ariel with him to his parents' house. He knew that his father might pass on that day.

Several days after "Poppy" died, Ariel did not want her favorite foods and did not want to drink out of her sippy cup. She said that she wanted the food, but when presented to her she did not eat it. Sometimes she would lick the food. She had started potty training before her grandfather's death but wanted the diaper again; in fact, she became constipated. An examination by a gastroenterologist indicated no physical problems. After Vinny's father died, when Ariel passed by "Poppy's" house, she stopped calling his name.

Two months later in May, Loretta's mother passed away. Ariel was close to her "Nanny" but did not mention her not visiting anymore. Loretta notes that Ariel had some fears before witnessing the death of Vinny's father. She was afraid of loud noises, thunder, blinds moving in the wind, noise from the lawn mover, and planes flying overhead. She was also afraid of unfamiliar faces and had difficulty sleeping. She began waking up every three hours. She helps in getting herself dressed, lets Loretta know if her diaper is soiled, and is proud when she accomplishes a task, yet she cries if Loretta leaves the room. She has advanced verbal skills, speaks in complete sentences, and communicates her needs accurately.

- What clinical tools might you consider to help the Russos?

  _____

  _____

- What do you think is going on with Ariel?

  _____

  _____

MINDFUL SELF-REFLECTION MOMENT
Close your eyes; take a breath.

What feelings or thoughts are you aware of?

_____

_____

_____

Assessment Guide for Small Children

Before assessment ask . . .

- What are your areas of concern for your child?

- Have you discovered any strategies or "little tricks" that are helpful when working with your child?

- Does your child have any favorite toys or activities that we could use during the assessment?

- Is there a special place or particular time of day that would be best to gather information about your child?

During assessment ask . . .

- Are we seeing a variety of things that your child can do?

- Is there another way that we could do this that might make your child participate or feel more comfortable?

- Would you like to show us some of the things you do with your child?

- Are we correctly interpreting what your child says and does?

After assessment ask. . .

- Were these typical behaviors and responses from your child?

- Do you feel that we were able to get an accurate picture of your child?

- Were there any other skills or behaviors that you would like us to see?

- Were we able to address your areas of concern?

(in Brink, M., 2002, p. 254)

Children Who Experience Death

Age of Child	Response to Death	Suggestion for Caregivers
Birth to three	Awareness that something is wrong, sensitivity to the emotional responses of the adults around them.	Keep routines as normal as possible. Be aware that a parent of a primary caregiver may be emotionally unavailable for the child. Understand that a child may regress to former behavior such as bedwetting.

Willis, 2002, p. 225.

THOUGHTS TO PONDER

There are variations on the two most common eating disorders found in adults, anorexia and bulimia. The disorders most commonly found in children are selective eating, food avoidance emotional disorder, and pervasive refusal syndrome (Bryant-Waugh and Lask, 1995).

Celebrating Family Culture

Vinny and Loretta are second-generation Italian Americans. Vinny's grandparents emigrated in the early 1920s from Milano, Italy. Loretta's grandparents emigrated from Sicily, Italy. Loretta's family were farmers, and Vinny's family were clothing manufacturers. Vinny and Loretta were raised with large extended families and "paisanos," close friends of the family who ranked the status of family. The fact that their families emigrated from different regions in Italy posed an additional layer of cultural norms. It is not unusual today for Italians from different regions to "intermarry," yet it is often met with disapproval from the family.

Loretta viewed Vinny's Milanese family as rigid and quiet in comparison to her Sicilian family, who were demonstrative and vocal. Loretta prided herself as a gourmet cook and was excited to cook large creative meals for Vinny's family. Due to their different traditional eating patterns, Vinny's family often did not eat the food she prepared; in addition, they voiced their opinion about how she spent money and how she raised the children. Vinny enjoyed the music, laughter, and company of Loretta's family, who liked to joke and were less serious than his family.

In spite of intracultural differences, Loretta and Vinny raised their family and were comfortable with Loretta's role as homemaker while Vinny supported the family financially. In traditional Italian households, gender roles are often specific and the women are expected to stay at home and manage the children and household affairs even though the husband usually has final authority over decisions. Loretta remembers a conversation with her grandmother before her marriage in which her grandmother advised her that "when you marry you no longer go out and have fun; the woman stays home, cares for the house and children. Always remember your place; this will earn the respect of your husband and his family." The Russos abided by this tradition, yet Loretta felt rejected when Vinny made major decisions without her consent.

In traditional Italian families, children are expected to please adults and are often not asked their opinions. The children's emotions are often not taken seriously. In the case of Ariel, Vinny and his family felt that Ariel was too young to have had any reaction to her grandfather's death, while Loretta's family felt the death could be the cause of Ariel's regression. This difference of opinion created more stress in the situation. Vinny's family told Loretta to take away Ariel's bottle, which would then force her to eat when she was hungry. Loretta's family advised Loretta to keep the bottle to assure nourishment. Loretta was conscious of not disrespecting Vinny and his family, and she knew the importance of "keeping quiet" to "uphold the respect" (an inherent cultural norm to agree with figures of authority and not question their advice). For example, Loretta tells a story about her aunt Carol, who at fifty years old would hide in the bathroom and smoke a cigarette to avoid her father's disapproval.

- What challenges might Vinny and Loretta face due to their differences?

_____

_____

- How might their similarities enhance their relationship and childrearing?

  _____

  _____

- How have the cultural and intracultural norms impacted Loretta and Vinny's life?

  _____

  _____

TAKE A ONE-MINUTE VACATION

Neck Stretches. Press head away from shoulders, gently tilting head backward so chin aims at ceiling. Then bring chin forward, pressing against the chest. Feel the back of the neck open and stretch. Bring head to center, tilting it to the left, lowering the ear toward the left shoulder. Turn head slightly to the side and slowly roll it back to center and then repeat on the right side. Feel the neck extend as you lean to each side. Remember to breathe throughout the stretch.

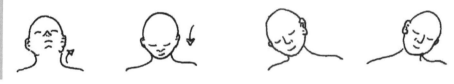

THERAPISTS' TOOLS

Children are the gauge of family function. They tell a clear story based on their symptoms and behavior of what is going on in the family. Engaging the child requires the therapist to see and explore the world through a "child's eyes," playful, spontaneous, and sometimes silly. In working with the Russos, the therapist needs to come out of the practical mode and allow curiosity to soar. "You have to have something strange, already in yourself, you have to be invasive, interested, and curious to enter other people's life. I think that is a basic requirement which I think is inside you and is part of your own family history. Then of course, you can practice or you can enlarge this curiosity or you can refine that" (Barketta, 2001, pp. 242–243).

In working with Ariel, the therapist will begin to realize the relationship issues between Loretta and Vinny and how that relationship ties them to their history. Therapists are like anthropologists "digging" into the past to see how it relates to the present and how it will impact the future.

Andolf discusses the importance of humor in therapy; he says "humor creates empathy," and he reflects upon Winnicott's early observation in working with children that therapists are often too serious and do not play enough and could become quite boring in their language and conversation. Difficult and important messages can be communicated to families by telling a joke. "If you are able to, get on the floor and play with kids as this sends a message to the adults . . . [that] it is much more useful and respectful than to stay on the chair so well educated" (Barletta, 2001, p.252). Let's explore how we can use curiosity, play, and humor in working with the Russos.

> *Curiosity.* Take yourself out of a particular theoretical framework, and allow yourself to be completely open to the mysteries that lie beneath the surface of the Russo's experience. To help you explore the history of the Russos, you must first be curious about yourself and learns about how your thoughts, bodies, and reactions emerge. Know when you are feeling constricted and rigid and closing yourself off to the magic of seeing events in a new way, "from a child's eyes."
>
> *Play.* Think about ways the family could play together. For example, ask the Russo family to sit on the floor or at a table with blocks, furniture, and dolls, and ask them to build a house together. The session can include Chelsea and Joanna giving their input and feelings to what's been going on. Observe the interactions among all members, ask questions, and allow them to share their thoughts and ideas.
>
> *Humor.* Too often therapists refrain from letting their humanity reveal itself. Tears and laughter are innate tools that convey a message to the family that you are comfortable with your own vulnerability. When we can "let go," it is at that moment that we make a deeper connection with the family. Try telling a funny story or bring humor into the session by addressing difficult issues with a lighter tone.

Riding the Wave

Loretta, Vinny, Ariel, and the therapist are in the therapist's office. The therapist has met several times with Loretta and Vinny. There are lots of toys scattered around. Ariel is sitting on Loretta's lap, clutching onto her.

THERAPIST: (Greets Vinny and Loretta and addresses Ariel, bending toward her.) Hi, Ariel; would you like to come over here and play with the puzzles?

ARIEL: (Reluctantly slides off Loretta's lap and walks toward therapist, looking back at parents, and takes *The Lion King* puzzle.)

THERAPIST: You can sit here at the play table. (Near therapist yet still can see parents.)

LORETTA: What a nice job you did finishing the puzzle.

ARIEL: (Smiles; Ariel likes *The Lion King*.)

THERAPIST: (Has a bowl of strawberries—Ariel's favorite food—on the table.) Would you like to give mom and dad a strawberry? (Ariel smiles broadly and takes two to her parents.)

ARIEL: (Looks at therapist and holds another strawberry with arm outstretched.)

THERAPIST: Is that one for me?

ARIEL: (Gives the strawberry to therapist.)

THERAPIST: (Looks at Loretta.) Do you think Ariel would like a strawberry?

LORETTA: Ariel, take a strawberry; it's your favorite.

ARIEL: (Looks at mom and smiles.)

VINNY: (Takes a strawberry and licks it and takes small bites. Ariel giggles. Vinny gives Ariel a strawberry.)

ARIEL: (Takes it and licks it, seemingly enjoying the texture and taste, yet does not eat it. She puts it down.)

LORETTA AND VINNY: Yummy!

- Describe how therapy is different with children than with adults.

  _____

  _____

- What skills does a therapist need in working with children?

  _____

  _____

Exploratory Research and Resource Corner

- What homework might you explore for the Russos?

  _____

  _____

• What resources might you explore to help you in treating the Russos?

_____

_____

Second Session: Loretta, Vinny, Ariel, and Therapist

The next session takes place two weeks later. Since then, Loretta's mother passed away. It's been a very difficult time for her since her mother died unexpectedly from a heart attack. Loretta depended upon her mother's support in dealing with Ariel and deeply felt her loss. Loretta's family is religious. Loretta has a bottle of holy water in Ariel's room that was given to her by her mother at Ariel's baptism. After many sleepless nights and two months of Ariel not eating, Loretta took the holy water and sprinkled it around Ariel and prayed to her deceased mother for Ariel to eat a pancake, her favorite breakfast food. Loretta kissed Ariel and went to sleep. The next morning at breakfast, Ariel asked for a pancake. Loretta prepared the food yet didn't pay much attention as Ariel often asked for her favorite foods but did not eat. This time she ate three pancakes. Loretta called all of her family and told the story about her prayer and holy water. Everyone understood, as each member felt their mother's presence since her death. Loretta felt that her mother helped Ariel, and Ariel has been eating since that day. Loretta believes that her mother's intervention and spirit motivated Ariel to eat.

• What are your thoughts about Loretta's spiritual experience and Ariel's desire to eat?

_____

_____

The session begins

VINNY: (Turns to the therapist before entering the room and smiles.) We have some good news. (He whispers.) Ariel has begun eating again!

THERAPIST: How wonderful! (They all enter the room, which is set up for a tea party, with tiny cups and saucers and snacks to eat, strawberries and melon, Ariel's favorites. Loretta and Vinny sit at the small table with the therapist; Ariel follows and is sitting next to mom, but not clutching today.)

LORETTA: (Begins the session by pouring an imaginary cup of tea.)

ARIEL: Daddy wants a cup of tea? (he responds; she pours. She then turns to therapist.) Want a cup of tea? (therapist responds and Ariel pours her a cup, too.)

VINNY: May I have a piece of fruit? (Vinny takes some strawberries.)

THERAPIST: The fruit is for all of us to share.

LORETTA: (Takes a piece of melon.)

ARIEL: (Takes a piece of melon and a strawberry.)

THERAPIST: (Takes a piece of melon and asks Ariel if she likes the fruits. Ariel eats the fruit and licks her lips in enjoyment.)

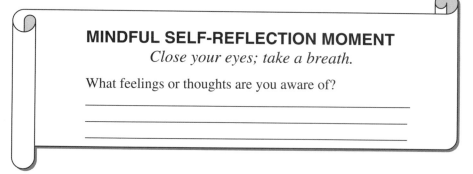

MINDFUL SELF-REFLECTION MOMENT
Close your eyes; take a breath.

What feelings or thoughts are you aware of?

_____

_____

_____

Beyond Treatment

The Russos are happy with the outcome now that Ariel is eating. They have been through many emotional and family changes in the past year and have had challenges prior to the death of Vinny's father and Loretta's mother.

- As the therapist working with this family, what would be your next step?

  _____

  _____

- What are the issues that remain with Loretta and Vinny both individually and as a couple?

  _____

  _____

• What services would you offer to the Russo family?

_____

_____

REFERENCES

Barletta, J. (2001). An uncommon family therapist: A conversation with Maurizio Andolfi. *Contemporary Family Therapy, 23*(2), 241–258.

Bryant-Waugh, R., & Lask, B. (1995). Eating disorders in children. *Journal of Child Psychology and Psychiatry and Allied Disciplines, 36*(3), 191–202.

Edmunds, H., & Hill, A. J. (1999). Dieting and the family contest of eating in young adolescent children. *International Journal of Eating Disorders. 25*(4), 435–440.

Ford, J. (1995). Wonderful ways to love a child, Conari Press, Berkely, CA.

Mahler, Pine and Bergman. The Psychological birth of the human infant: symbiosis and individuation. Basic Books Inc, NY. 39–120

Mariachi, M., & Cohen, P. (1990). Early childhood eating behaviors and adolescent eating disorders. *Journal of the American Academy of Child and Adolescent Psychiatry, 29*(1), 112–117.

Willis, C. A. (2002). The grieving process in children: Strategies for understanding, educating and reconciling children's perceptions of death. *Early Childhood Education Journal, 29*(4), 221–226.

SUGGESTED READING

Birth to Three System, www.birth23.org, an early intervention program.

Brink, M. B. (2002). Involving parents in early childhood assessment: Perspectives from an early intervention instructor. *Early Childhood Education Journal, 29*(4), 251–257.

Christian, L. G. (1997). Children and death. *Young Children, 52*(4), 76–80.

Lalli, M. (1969). The Italian-American family: Assimilation and change, 1900–1965. *The Family Coordinator, 18*(1), 44–48.

Lantz, J., & Ahern, R. (1998). Re-collection in existential psychotherapy with couples and families dealing with death. *Contemporary Family Therapy, 20*(1), 47–57.

McKeever, P. (1980). When Jason's grandpa died: The response of a toddler to the events surrounding the death of a grandparent. *Essence, 4*(1), 19–24.

McWilliam, R. A., & Scott, S. (2001). A support approach to early intervention: A three-part framework. *Infants and Young Children, 13*(4), 55–66.

Morgan, M. L., & Wampler, K. S. (2003). Fostering client creativity in family therapy: A process research study. *Contemporary Family Therapy, 25*(2), 207–228.

Norris-Shorstle, C., Young, P. A., & Williams, M. A. (1993). Understanding death and grief for children three and younger. *Social Work, 38*(6), 736–742.

Ponterotto, J. G., Rao, V., Zweig, J., Reiger, B. P., Schaefer, K., Michaelakou, S., et al. (2001). The relationship of acculturation and gender attitudes toward counseling in Italian and Greek American college students. *Cultural Diversity and Ethnic Minority Psychology,* November, 362–375.

Saionte-Strumolo, N., & Dunn, A. B. (2000). Consideration of cultural and relational issues in bereavement: The case of an Italian American Family. *Family Journal· Counseling and Therapy for Couples and Families, 8*(4), 334–400.

10

Keep One Kidney for Me, Please: The Story of the Kashanis

The sheer inability to hide from illness, to permanently trade its embrace for
that of health, might tell us about the relationship of the two: that they are
mysteriously united in some odd way; that to know one is to know the other;
that one cannot have one without having the other. Just as one cannot know
up without down, or black without white, it appears that we cannot partition
our awareness in a way that excludes illness and death in favor of health.

Zweig and Abrams, 1991, p. 92

Getting Started

CONSTANCE: Dr. Hazelhurst strongly suggested that I see a professional who specializes in solid organ transplants, and he highly recommended you.

THERAPIST: What is the nature of the referral?

CONSTANCE: (Defiant and angry.) I have no idea; he just told me to call you.

THERAPIST: You don't sound happy about this at all; it's helpful to enter counseling with some motivation. What's going on?

CONSTANCE: (Bluntly responds.) Why don't you call him and find out?

What reactions are you aware of right now?

_____

_____

Constance, a sixteen-year-old Iranian American voluntarily showed up in the emergency room of a well-known Los Angeles hospital after partying with her friends earlier in the evening. Her best friend Shayla was frightened when Constance remarked that she thought she was having a heart attack. Constance had shortness of breath, sharp, striking pain near and around her chest, numbness on one side, and hyperventilation.

Following a call to Constance's nephrologist (Constance was a transplant candidate), test results revealed positive high levels of cocaine. This development could discredit Constance from transplant candidacy. Simply stated, without a transplant Constance would not live.

• What are your initial thoughts about Constance?

_____

_____

• How would you proceed as a therapist working with Constance?

_____

_____

• What do you know about transplant patients?

_____

_____

Session with Therapist, Dr. Hazelhurst, Constance,
and Elly and Sammy Kashani

Dr. Hazelhurst was a leading pediatric nephrologist who first spoke with Constance alone to discuss the positive drug test. She was upset, yet Dr. Hazelhurst felt that bringing everyone together to discuss where to go from here was critical since Constance was on the transplant list for a kidney.

DR. HAZELHURST: (To Elly & Sammy) It has come to our attention that Constance tested positive for cocaine.

SAMMY AND ELLY: (Looking shocked and bewildered.) I can't believe this is true!

CONSTANCE: (Defensive.) It's not true! Dr. Hazelhurst has it out for me and made it up!

DR. HAZELHURST: Constance, we have the test results right here (Shows her the results.) and we need to discuss what we can do since this will impact the team's decision of your candidacy for a kidney transplant.

ELLY: Constance, please, is this true?

CONSTANCE: (Defensively.) No, I said, I did not use cocaine!

THERAPIST: Constance, I realize how difficult this must be for you knowing how important it is for you to have a new kidney, yet we have a chance to look at what happened with the cocaine. We all make mistakes. Can we meet privately and talk some more about this and plan together?

CONSTANCE: (Looks down at the floor.) I guess so.

SAMMY: We need to know what's going on; I think we should all meet.

THERAPIST: It would be helpful if Constance and I met alone; maybe I can meet with the both of you after I meet with Constance. (Therapist turns to Constance.) Would that be all right with you?

CONSTANCE: I'll think about it. Maybe it would be OK if you talk to them.

- How would you proceed from here as the therapist working with Constance?

  _____

  _____

- What might Sammy and Elly Corbin be experiencing as Constance's parents?

  _____

  _____

- Discuss the issues surrounding organ transplant for the patient and family.

_____

_____

A Window into the Past

Constance

Constance was born a twin. She and her brother Hershel were born several weeks premature. Constance's kidney problems started when she was born. Her kidneys simply did not develop in utero to mature into fully functioning organs. Hershel's kidneys, on the other hand, matured fully and he did not have any of the problems Constance had. Hershel grew up experiencing all the normal developmental stages of a young boy's life while his sister spent her toddler and childhood years in and out of the hospital undergoing many surgical procedures to try and correct the dysfunctional organs. She was often placed on dialysis when her kidneys would stop functioning completely. Growing up in this environment predisposed her to taking the role of being "the weak or sick one." As a child, she needed assistance conducting all of her activities of daily living. As she matured into adolescent years, she continued to rely heavily on her parents for everything, and they readily continued to adopt the role of her personal caretakers. There was much focus on Constance due to her health, and her health took precedence over everything. In fact, everyone in the Corbin family performed their role so well that Constance grew up learning how not to take responsibility for her thoughts, feelings, or actions. She was quite literally the "center of attention" in the family.

Hershel

With much focus being placed on Constance, there was little time left to develop relationships among the other family members. Constance's brother Hershel became invisible and felt left out. He worried about Constance and became accustomed to meeting his own needs. He saw how concerned and exhausted his parents were and felt guilty to ask for attention; he did not want to increase their burden. Hershel spent his days on the basketball courts after school and over at his friends' houses as a way of remaining invisible to his family. He felt ashamed of having a healthy body as his twin sister and family focused constantly on the weakness and fragility of her body.

- What are your thoughts about Constance's early development?

_____

_____

- How would you address Constance's dependency?

  _____

  _____

- What are your thoughts about Hershel? Would you include him in treatment?

  _____

  _____

- What are some of the issues confronting siblings of chronically ill children?

  _____

  _____

Elly

Elly is a 40 year old Persian/Iranian American woman who is the youngest of four sibling, two older brothers and one older sister. She and her family are practicing Baha'is. The core belief of Bahism is the unity of all religions and all people are one. Her family emigrated from Tehran, Iran to Illinois in the United States in 1968. Tehran is the capital of Iran and also the political, economic and intellectual capital of Iran. For many years the family sold collectible art and Persian rugs. Elly's extended family are intellectuals and all were raised in the Baha'i faith. Her family left Iran fearing persecution due to rejection of those who practiced Baha'i. She worked in her family's antique shops and traveled internationally as a buyer of unusual artifacts for the business. She met Sammy when she was 22 years old through her brother who was his college roommate. The relationship was accepted by both families since they were both Persian/Iranian and practiced Baha'i. Elly sees her parents and family often. She has a large extended family and gatherings are a major part of her life.

Sammy

Sammy is 47 years old and the oldest of five siblings, three brothers and a sister. Sammy and his family are practicing Baha'i's. His family emigrated to Illinois in the United States in 1969. They lived in Tehran and were investment bankers. They continued in banking after they emigrated to the United States. Sammy worked in the family banking business after graduating college. Although Sammy has a large family, they don't see each other as often as he sees Elly's family. His parents travel extensively for pleasure and business yet there is much festivity with his parents, siblings and extended family during religious celebrations. His younger sister of 32 and older brother of 45 live near by. Elly and Sammy are close to them and see each other often.

Elly and Sammy

Elly and Sammy were married two years after Elly graduated from college. They have enjoyed the privileges of a comfortable lifestyle due to Sammy's family's banking business and Elly's family's antique business. Their families emigrated to the United States from Tehran in the late 1960s to escape religious persecution. During their early relationship, Elly and Sammy enjoyed playing tennis, golfing, and traveling to interesting places. They had much in common culturally, enjoyed each other's friends and family and felt they had a strong marriage. Both Sammy and Elly's families are philanthropists and contribute large sums of money to the Peace Corps, the American Kidney Association, various educational institutions and other charitable organizations. They respect each other as equals, value education, are accepting of other cultures and religions and are environmentalists. These values are a core component of their Baha'i faith.

Elly & Sammy's relationship became very estranged due to the challenges of dealing with Constance. In fact, it became apparent that Constance had become a surrogate partner to her father. Dad would often call Constance to check in several times a day and share with her his day-to-day personal business. Constance loved her father's attention and took on an almost "giddy" response when her dad called to find out how her day was going. She had her father "wrapped around her little finger," as her girlfriends would say. He organized his weekends around her activities and turned down social activities with Elly or friends "just in case Constance might have a medical emergency" and need him. When Constance did not "need" Sammy, he would busy himself in work. He never attended a basketball game in which Hershel played, nor did he show much interest in his son's athletic accomplishments.

Elly did not seem to mind the attention Sammy gave Constance; in fact, she took comfort in her martyrdom because it provided refuge for her unresolved guilt for not being able to keep gestation full term. Inside, she secretly felt that Constance's condition was all her fault. Her secret guilt caused her great inner turmoil that was relieved only when she could provide a caretaking role to Constance.

- What's going on with Sammy? Elly?

_____

_____

- How might the change in lifestyle due to Constance's illness affect both Sammy and Elly?

_____

_____

- Discuss issues faced by parents of children who are experiencing or waiting for transplantation.

- Describe what you would do at this point in treatment.

Embracing the Essence

Sessions with Constance, Sammy, and Elly

The Kashanis were sitting in the waiting room. Sammy and Constance sat on a sofa by themselves. Mom sat nearby in a chair. The therapist asked if she could see Constance alone at first, and asked Constance if this was okay. Constance hesitantly agreed. Her physical appearance was that of a petite twelve-year-old girl instead of a sixteen-year-old. She was very small, and her physical appearance was childlike. She had red scars and blisters (a common sign of a dialysis patient) in varying degrees of healing, and she wore a turtleneck sweater. The therapist asked Constance to choose wherever she would like to sit and ignored her glaring stare of distrust as the door was closing.

> **THERAPIST:**   (Breaking the ice, warmly welcomes Constance.) Before we begin, I would like to go over some housekeeping items, confidentiality, and releases of information. (Therapist talks about setting goals together and offers Constance the opportunity to ask questions along the way.) Hopefully we can form a connection and decide to work together.

> **CONSTANCE:**   (Tightens her jaw.) I want to know what kind of spy you are. Are you planning to investigate why I am here and tell Dr. Hazlehurst everything so that I end up not getting a kidney transplant?

> **THERAPIST:**   Even though Dr. Hazlehurst and the transplant team asked you to call, I am not a spy, and I do hope we can begin to develop trust. It's true that I will be asked to write a letter explaining our goals and accomplishments, but I plan for us to set up the goals together. The lifestyle and choices you make will greatly affect your eligibility for a new kidney.

CONSTANCE: (Crying at this point.) I need the transplant to live! I've been telling everyone in my family for years I needed to see someone. They don't believe in shrinks. They think all I have to do is talk to one of them and things will be OK. My parents are so upset about what I've done. This is such a mess. (Constance continues to cry for some time.)

THERAPIST: (Waits for Constance to compose herself.) My interest is in seeing you get the transplant. I know this feels very overwhelming, but often it takes a crisis for an opportunity to happen. If it were not for your positive drug test, you may never have been given the opportunity to see a therapist. I propose that we make a plan together and work toward ways of resolving some of these issues. Now. Let's see how I can be helpful to you.

(Sammy and Elly join the session. Therapist informs them that Constance will continue with therapy and every effort will be made to recommend the transplant.)

- What clinical tools would help you deal with Constance at this point?

_____

_____

- What would be your next step in treatment?

_____

_____

Exploratory Research and Resource Corner

- What might you need to know if you visited a nearby hospital and met with a nurse, physician, or social worker from a transplant team?

_____

_____

- What homework assignment might you explore with Constance?

_____

_____

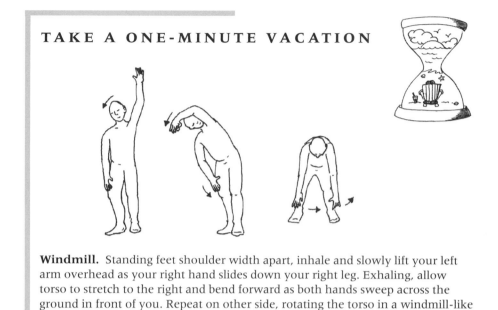

TAKE A ONE-MINUTE VACATION

Windmill. Standing feet shoulder width apart, inhale and slowly lift your left arm overhead as your right hand slides down your right leg. Exhaling, allow torso to stretch to the right and bend forward as both hands sweep across the ground in front of you. Repeat on other side, rotating the torso in a windmill-like

Celebrating Family Culture

Elly and Sammy have enjoyed a privileged lifestyle, yet they have endured historical suffering due to the persecution of their family in Tehran and the emotional pain of their daughter Constance. "The Baha'i faith, an offshoot of Islam, originated in Iran 150 years ago and claims more than five million members around the world including thousands in Iran, where it is officially rejected as a wayward sect" (Gollust, 2005). "The Baha'i faith is still regarded by many Muslims as a breakaway sect of Islam. Baha'is are heavily persecuted in some countries, particularly Iran." (http://www.religioustoler-ance.org//bahai.htm) Morphew (1998) reports that "there is no question now that the Bahai's who live in Iran are in for severe persecution by their government." Morphew notes that the government has set up declarations to prevent the progress of Baha'i by expelling them from universities, destroying their cultural roots, denying them employment and positions in education. Elly and Sammy worry about their extended family and hope to find ways to help them escape. They send packages of clothing, money and other things they may need to survive.

Moore and Shellman (2004) discuss the fear of persecution and forced migration. They studied migration using a global sample over more than forty years 1952-1995 and found that "violent behavior has a substantively larger impact on forced migration than variables such as the type of political institute or the average size of the economy" (p. 723). "In short, one will leave one's home when the probability of being a victim of persecution becomes sufficiently higher than the expected and the utility of leaving exceed the expected utility of staying" (p. 727). Years ago, many people left their countries for better economic opportunity. Today the high incidence of persecution in many countries have forced people to leave their homes, businesses, families and friends. Elly and Sammy continue in prayer with their families and friends in the United States in hopes that their Baha'i family and friends are safe and can escape persecution.

The idea of organ transplant is relatively new, and the research for understanding the etiology and psychosocial aspects of transplant dates began in the 1990s. Research for children and adolescents is even scarcer. Constance is confronted with the chaotic developmental milestones of adolescence compounded with the physical and psychological scars from her chronic kidney failure. Her anger and defensive nature is an impairment at this time while she waits for a kidney. Her brother being a gifted athlete and not having any physical challenges only compounds Constance's feelings of weakness and anger.

Penkower, Dew, Ellis, Sereika, Kitutu, and Shapiro (2003) studied twenty-two renal transplant recipient adolescents thirteen to eighteen years old. They found that adolescents with excessive anger were at greater risk for failure to adhere to the medical regimen (failure to take medications, failure to do required monthly blood work, and failure to attend clinic appointments regularly) than those who did not display excessive anger. The researchers found that as time progressed, parents had more difficulty monitoring adherence to medication regimen. It was hypothesized that as adolescents increased in age, they sought more autonomy from parents and gave less control to parents to monitor the necessary treatment.

Manificat, Dzord, Cochat, Morin, Plainguet, and Debray (2003) found in their quality-of-life (QOL) study with transplant children and adolescents "concern about their body or health, less pleasure than ordinary adolescents to manage by themselves and a poor relationship with peers. Mothers indicated a deep impact of the child's illness on their own quality of life, and the need for psychological support" (p. 228).

The issue of QOL is critical in working with transplant patients. "The definition of [QOL] is patients centered as opposed to physiological measurements and may encompass clinical, psychological, socioeconomic or even spiritual nuances" (Joseph, Baines, Morris, & Jindal, 2003, p. 431). The principal assessment tools used for evaluating candidates for transplantation are as follows:

The Psychosocial Assessment of Candidates for Transplantation (PACT). Assesses substance abuse, compliance, social support, lifestyle, and understanding of the transplantation process

The Psychosocial Levels System (PLS). Assesses coping skills based on psychiatric history, affect, mental health statutes, support, and anxiety

Transplant Evaluation Rating Scale (TERS). Evaluates ten psychosocial aspects of patient functions and is an expansion of the PLS

Sharkey and Gourishanker (2003) found that a multidisciplinary educational program for patients awaiting kidney transplantation increased patients' and their families' desire to receive complete information prior to renal transplantation so they could make an informed decision. Therapists working with families who have an adolescent experiencing transplantation need to understand the etiology of the process as well as the socioeconomic, psychological, and emotional challenges that face both the family members and the transplant patient.

- What cultural and lifestyle challenges have impacted the Kashanis?

  _____

  _____

- What are your thoughts about religious persecution and the impact it may have on the Kashanis?

  _____

  _____

THERAPISTS' TOOLS

The goal of therapy is to bring congruence of thoughts, feelings, and actions. Often experiences, particularly painful ones, take us out of harmony due to fear, anger, abandonment, and a host of other emotions that prevent us from feeling integrated. The Kashanis are stuck in a cycle of dancing around Constance's illness, hence cutting off family members from maintaining and developing homeostasis. How can you help the Kashanis to be more connected to their individual feelings, thoughts, and body awareness with so much time invested in focusing on the fear of losing Constance and Constance's fear of death? Let's look at how you, as the therapist, can create a safe environment to facilitate the process of self-discovery and inner wisdom for members of the Kashani family.

1. *Inner-body sensations.* Help each family member become aware of how the body feels in the moment, including breath, muscles, ligaments, and energy.
2. *Sensory perception.* Help each family member focus on inner and outer sensory functions, smell, taste, sight, touch, hearing, instinct, and body temperature.
3. *Movement.* Help each family member become aware of how his or her body responds to the present experience, from micromovement to large motor movement, including posture changes, facial expressions, and gestures.

4. *Affective states.* Help each family member focus on emotions such as fear or joy and notice how those feelings are experienced. For example, anger may be experienced as a feeling of peace, and joy as irritation, the opposite of what we may expect. Each individual has his or her own imprint of how he or she experiences emotions based on personal life events.

5. *Cognition.* Help each family member observe how his or her thoughts, meanings, and interpretation of events impact what is happening in his or her life (Ogden, 1996). Helping the Kashanis develop congruence and integration of the inner and outer reality can be enhanced by creating a safe and gentle environment during the exploration process of therapy.

TAKE A ONE-MINUTE VACATION

Pay attention to your breath; enjoy a few stretches, notice how your body feels; hold the stretch; and let go.

MINDFUL SELF-REFLECTION MOMENT
Close your eyes; take a breath.

What feelings or thoughts are you aware of?

_____

_____

_____

Riding the Wave

Session with Therapist and Constance

During the last session with Constance, Constance revealed how she resented the role of the "sick" one in the family. She felt sorry for her mother's guilt about not carrying her to full term and hides her feelings from her mother by avoiding her. She resented her dependency upon her parents and discussed how emotionally and physically drained she felt after dialysis, needing their help, feeling sick, nauseous, and unable to move afterward. She discussed prior drug abuse (mushrooms, speed, methamphetamine) and how she wanted to "party with her friends as a way of feeling normal—like everyone else." She indicated that she stopped using drugs at age fourteen and admitted that the recent cocaine abuse was a "stupid" thing to do.

Constance shared that her father had an affair with another woman when Constance was ten years old. It was a time when Constance was hospitalized and not expected to live. The girlfriend went to the hospital to see Constance "incognito" and pretended to be an old family friend but was met by Elly. unexpectedly. Constance indicated that her parents' relationship was never the same after that, but they never sought help. Constance was aware of the strained relationship between her parents.

Session with Constance, Sammy, Elly, and Hershel
following several sessions with therapist and Constance alone.

THERAPIST: I'm glad we are all here together. Hopefully we can use this time to begin communicating with each other.

ELLY: I see a change in Constance's attitude. I wonder how things are going?

THERAPIST: (Turns to Constance.)

CONSTANCE: I have made some decisions about my life. I am going to stop using all drugs except the ones prescribed for me. I am going to start going to teen AA meetings, and I want to start being honest with all of you.

SAMMY: I'm impressed with your progress, Constance. How can we help?

CONSTANCE: I'm trying to take some responsibility for myself and not play the victim all the time. I know I have a serious illness, yet there are some healthy parts of me too, physically and mentally.

HERSHEL: I'm so glad to hear this; you always see yourself as so weak, but I see your strong determination and will. Maybe now that you are taking some control of your own life, all of you can focus some time on me and what's happening in my life! For example, why doesn't anyone in this family ever go to my games?

ELLY: Have I failed you too, Hershel?

HERSHEL: You always seem to feel so bad about Constance, I don't tell you anything!

SAMMY: (Steps in.) You know how much attention Constance has needed.

CONSTANCE: (Looks at Hershel.) I'm sorry you have been left out so much, Hershel. I always assumed that because you were so healthy that you were okay. Now I know that health comes in all forms, physical, mental, and emotional. I would like to spend some time with you, Hershel, and hear more about what's going on in your life. You are right—you have accomplished a lot and I have been way too focused on myself to pay attention to you or anyone else! I bet you are an amazing athlete!

ELLY AND SAMMY: (To Hershel.) I think we have ignored you way too long!

ELLY: (Looks at her husband.) I have been holding onto a lot of resentment toward you since your affair. I think it's time to do something about it. I'm tired of feeling bad all the time.

SAMMY: I don't think this is the time or place to discuss this issue.

THERAPIST: I would be happy to give you some names of therapists that can help you both.

ELLY: Thank you.

CONSTANCE: (Turning to parents.) I know that I've needed you both and still do, but seeing the tension between you hurts almost as much as my illness. I want you two to get help and work things out.

SAMMY: I'm glad that you are telling me how you feel and how you are taking charge, growing up. You have taught me something today.

CONSTANCE: I guess I have something to offer you and mom, too.

THERAPIST: Maybe we can all meet next week. (To Sammy and Elly.) I will give you some names before you leave. (Turning to Hershel.) Would you like to come to therapy next week?

HERSHEL: Yes, this helped me see things more clearly and finally speak my truth.

THERAPIST: See you next week.

(Elly walks out with Constance and Hershel walks out with Sammy.)

• What are your thoughts about Constance's sense of independence?

_____

_____

• What interventions might you explore with Hershel?

_____

_____

- What changes in the home might you explore with the Kashanis at this point in treatment?

_____

_____

Beyond Treatment

Constance was progressing very well with her commitment to sobriety and lifestyle changes. She grew in strength, confidence, and assertiveness. She joined the therapist in writing the letter to the transplant team and was received well. The team noticed that Constance seemed to have a "new" respect for what was to transpire with the kidney transplant. Sammy and Elly decided to begin counseling, and Hershel joined several more family sessions.

- What would be the next step for the Kashanis in treatment, if any?

_____

_____

- Discuss your thoughts about what the Kashanis can do to move them along their path of transformation.

_____

_____

MINDFUL SELF-REFLECTION MOMENT
Close your eyes; take a breath.

What feelings or thoughts are you aware of?

_____

_____

_____

REFERENCES

Gollust, D. (2005). US condemns persecution of Iranian religious captive who died in prison. *VOA news* December 23rd Washington.

Hatcher, W. S. J. & Martin, D. (2003) The Baha'i Faith: The Emerging Global Religion, Wilmette, Ill, and Baha'i Publishing Trust. http://www.religioustolerance.org//bahai.htm

Joseph, J. T., Baines, L. S., Morris, M. C., & Jindal, R. M. (2003). Quality of life after kidney and pancreas transplantation: A review. *American Journal of Kidney Diseases, 42*(3), 431–445.

Moore, W. H. & Shellman, S. M. (2004) Fear of Persecution: forced migration, 1952-1995. *Journal of Conflict Resolution* 40 (5) 723–745.

Morphew, C. (1998) Persecution said to grow harsher for Iranian Bahai's Knight Ridder Newspapers Thursday, November 5th.

Ogden, P. (1996) Hands on Psychotherapy. *Hakomi Journal,* Issue 12 Summer

Penkower, L., Dew, M. A., Ellis, D., Sereika, S. M., Kitutu, J. M. M., & Shapiro, R. (2003). Psychological distress and adherence to the medical regimen among adolescent renal transplant recipients. *American Journal of Transplantation, 3,* 1418–1425.

Russo. S. A. & Lewis, J. E. (1999) The Cross-Cultural applications of the KAIT: case studies with three differentially acculturated women. *Cultural Diversity and Ethnic Minority Psychology* 5 (1) 76–85

Sharkey, C., & Gourishankar, S. (2003). Transplant friends: An interactive education program for patients awaiting kidney transplantation. *Transplantation Proceedings, 35,* 2405–2406.

Zweig, A., & Abrams, J. (1991). *Meeting the shadow: The hidden power of the dark side of human nature,* p. 92. New York: Penguin/Putnam Inc.

SUGGESTED READING

Cook, C. A., Becvar, D. S., & Pontious, S. L. (2000). Complementary alternative medicine in health and mental health: Implications for social work practice. *Social Work Health Care, 31*(3), 39–57.

Eiser, C. (1990). Psychological effects of chronic disease. *Journal of Child Psycho Psychiatry, 31*(1), 85–98.

Elder, C. R. (2004). Integrating natural medicine into conventional clinical practice: The example of vedic medicine. *Integrative Medicine: A Clinician's Journal, 3*(3), 18–23.

Engle, D. (2001). Psychosocial aspects of the organ transplant experience: What has been established and what we need for the future. *Journal of Clinical Psychology, 57*(4), 521–540.

Fennell, R. S., Tucker, C., & Pedersen, T. (2001). Demographic and medical predictors of medication compliance among ethnically different pediatric renal transplant patients. *Pediatric Transplant, 5,* 343–348.

Forsberg, A., Lorenzon, U., Nilsson, F., & Backmana, L. (1990). Pain and health related quality of life after heart, kidney and liver transplantation. *Clinical Transplantation, 13*(6), 453–460.

Griffin, K. J., & Elkin, T. D. (2001). Non-adherence in pediatric transplantation: A review of the existing literature. *Pediatric Transplant, 5,* 246–249

Lindqvist, R., Carlsson, M., & Sjoden, P. O. (2003). Coping strategies of people with kidney transplants. *Journal of Advanced Nursing, 45*(1), 47–52.

Manificat, S., Dazord, A., Cochat, P., Morin, D., Plainguet, F., & Debray, D. (2003). Quality of life of children and adolescents after kidney or liver transplantation: Child, parents and caregiver's point of view. *Pediatric Transplantation, 7,* 228–235.

Quinn, J. F., Smith, M., Ritenbaugh, C., Swanson, K.. & Watson, J. (2003). Research guidelines for assessing the impact of the healing relationship in clinical nursing. *Alternative Therapies, 9*(3), A65–A79.

Reynolds, J. M., Morton, M. J., Garralda, M. E., Postlewaite, R. J., & Goh, D. (1993). Psychosocial adjustment of adult survivors of a pediatric dialysis and transplant programme. *Arch Dis Child, 68,* 104–110.

Sayles, C. (2002). Transformation and change—Based on the model of Virginia Satir. *Comtemporary Family Therapy, 24*(1), 93–109.

Smith, J. M., & McDonald, R. A. (2000). Progress in renal transplantation for children. *Advanced Renal Replacement Therapy, 7*(2), 158–171.

Suris, J. C., Parera, N., & Puig, C. (1996). Chronic illness and emotional distress in adolescence. *Journal of Adolescent Health, 19,* 153–156.

Von Essen, L., Enskar, K., Dreuger, A., Larsson, B., & Sjoden, P. O. (2000). Self-esteem, depression and anxiety among Swedish children and adolescents on and off cancer treatment. *Acta Pediatrics, 89,* 229–236.

Weiner, M. D., Pentz, M. A., Turner, G. E., & Dwyer, J. H. (2001). From early to late adolescence: Alcohol use and anger relationships. *Journal of Adolescent Health, 28,* 450–457.